WESTERN VIEWS
OF ISLAM
IN THE MIDDLE AGES

WESTERN VIEWS OF ISLAM IN THE MIDDLE AGES

✳✳✳

R. W. Southern

HARVARD UNIVERSITY PRESS

CAMBRIDGE, MASSACHUSETTS · 1962

Publication of this book has been
aided by a grant from the Ford Foundation.

✤

Library of Congress Catalog Card Number 62–13270
Printed in the United States of America

TO
RICHARD HUNT

PREFACE

✳ ✳ ✳ ✳ ✳

THE invitation to give three lectures at Harvard in April of this year encouraged me to put into shape some thoughts on the problem of Islam as it was viewed in western Europe in the Middle Ages. I seized the opportunity with eagerness, and I owe a debt of gratitude to the History Department, and especially to Professor Robert L. Wolff, both for the invitation and for many other kindnesses. I have received much assistance from Islamic students in Oxford, especially from Dr. R. R. Walzer and Dr. S. M. Stern; and I should not have ventured on such a vast and confusing subject if a great deal of it had not recently been charted by Dr. N. Daniel in his learned volume *Islam and the West: The Making of an Image.* I do not pretend to emulate the learning of these scholars on Islamic matters; but I have tried to set Islam against the changing Western scene throughout the Middle Ages, and to revive the hopes and fears which it inspired. The experience is not irrelevant to us today.

R. W. S.

Oxford, 5 May 1961

CONTENTS

✳✳✳✳✳

WESTERN VIEWS
OF ISLAM
IN THE MIDDLE AGES

I

THE AGE OF IGNORANCE
❉❉❉❉❉❉❉❉❉❉❉❉❉❉❉❉❉❉❉❉

THE subject I have chosen deserves our attention, I think, for several reasons. In the first place, we have reached a point in the study of medieval history at which it is very important that attention should be directed to communities outside western Europe, and especially to those that exercised an influence on the development of the West. This, of course, is not a new idea. But it is one that has to struggle not only against great intrinsic difficulties but also against the conservatism of established academic routine. So far as Islam is concerned, it is only in quite recent years that its relations with medieval Christendom have been the subject of serious study. It is true that over a hundred years ago the French scholar Ernest Renan showed the way in one of the most perceptive and original works produced by the new historical movement of his day—I mean his volume on Averroes and Averroism.[1] But his example was not followed. The great historians of the late nineteenth and early twentieth centuries devoted

[1] E. Renan, *Averroès et l'Averroïsme*, 1852.

themselves primarily to the social, legal, and political growth of European countries, and it was not until the years between the two World Wars that a serious effort was made to understand the contribution of Islam to the development of Western thought, and the effect on Western society of the neighborhood of Islam.[2] Since that time, and especially since 1945, the work has gone vigorously forward, and it may be useful to take a general view of the whole field as it now stands revealed. It will soon become apparent that there are still many dark corners and some subjects which have scarcely yet been touched, though it may well be that some of this darkness is due to my own ignorance and not to the imperfect state of scholarship.

There is a second reason, and a less academic one, for directing our attention to this subject at this moment. The greatest practical problem of our time is the problem of the juxtaposition of incompatible and largely hostile systems of thought, morals, and belief embodied in political powers of impressive, not to say awe-inspiring, size. We sometimes talk as if this were a new problem, and certainly it is new to the modern world. The Western sense of superiority in every sphere of endeavor has scarcely been challenged for three hundred years. It has become part of our heritage, most painful to abandon or adjust. But western Europe went through all this painful experience

[2] I may mention especially U. Monneret de Villard, *Lo studio dell' Islam in Europa nel XII e nel XIII secola* (Studi e Testi, 110), 1944; G. Théry, *Tolède, grande ville de la Renaissance médiévale,* 1944; D. Cabanelas Rodriguez, *Juan de Segovia y el problema islamica,* 1952; N. Daniel, *Islam and the West: The Making of an Image,* 1960. The last of these works contains a full bibliography.

more than a thousand years ago, and lived with it as a more
or less permanent challenge to its complacency throughout
the Middle Ages. The existence of Islam was the most far-
reaching problem in medieval Christendom. It was a problem at every level of experience. As a practical problem it
called for action and for discrimination between the com-
peting possibilities of Crusade, conversion, coexistence, and
commercial interchange. As a theological problem it called
persistently for some answer to the mystery of its existence:
what was its providential role in history—was it a symptom
of the world's last days or a stage in the Christian development; a heresy, a schism, or a new religion; a work of
man or devil; an obscene parody of Christianity, or a system
of thought that deserved to be treated with respect? It was
difficult to decide among these possibilities. But before de-
ciding it was necessary to know the facts, and these were
not easy to know. So there arose an historical problem that
could not be solved, could scarcely be approached, without
linguistic and literary knowledge difficult to acquire, and
made more difficult by secrecy, prejudice, and the strong
desire not to know for fear of contamination.

In a word, medieval scholars and men of affairs came up
against all the problems with which, in a different context,
we are familiar. They asked many of the same questions
that we ask, and we may learn something from their
failures. The one thing we cannot expect to find in the
Middle Ages is that spirit of detached and academic or
humane inquiry which has characterized much of the inquiry about Islam of the last hundred years, whether in the
heroic journeys of Doughty or the impassioned prose of

Carlyle. This spirit of detachment was a product of superiority and of the conviction that there was nothing to fear. Hence an easy sympathy and regard. For the medieval observer there was too much at stake to permit this indulgence. I am reminded of a passage in the life of Dr. Johnson, in which a Mr. Murray praised the ancient philosophers for the candor and good humor of their philosophical differences, and Dr. Johnson retorted:

Sir, they disputed with good humour, because they were not earnest as to religion . . . when a man has nothing to lose, he may be in good humour with his opponent. . . . Being angry with one who controverts an opinion which you value is a necessary consequence of the uneasiness which you feel. Every man who attacks my belief diminishes in some degree my confidence in it, and therefore makes me uneasy; and I am angry with him who makes me uneasy.[3]

Dr. Johnson always responded with sympathy to the primitive emotions of mankind, and he accurately expresses the temper of the medieval dispute. The existence of Islam made the West profoundly uneasy. On the practical plane it caused permanent unease, not only because it was a danger but because the danger was unpredictable and immeasurable: the West had no access to the counsels or motives of Islam. But this incalculable factor was only an indication of a deeper incomprehension of the nature of the thing itself.

In understanding Islam, the West could get no help from antiquity, and no comfort from the present. For an age

[3] J. Boswell, *Life of Samuel Johnson,* ed. G. B. Hill and L. F. Powell, 1934–1940, III, 10–11.

avowedly dependent on the past for its materials, this was a serious matter. Intellectually the nearest parallel to the position of Islam was the position of the Jews. They shared many of the same tenets and brought forward many of the same objections to Christianity. But Christian thinkers had at their disposal an embarrassing wealth of material for answering the Jewish case; and the economic and social inferiority of the Jews encouraged the view that their case could be treated with disdain. Nothing is easier than to brush aside the arguments of the socially unsuccessful, and we can see this verified in the melancholy history of the Jewish controversy in the Middle Ages. The same mixture of social superiority with a long tradition of authoritative refutation was responsible for the confidence with which the medieval Church faced the many heresies which arose in Europe from the eleventh century onwards. Even the Greek schism could be pressed into this mold: wordly decline and patristic authority combined to lend each other mutual support.

But Islam obstinately resisted this treatment. It was immensely successful. Every period of incipient breakdown was succeeded by a period of astonishing and menacing growth. Islam resisted both conquest and conversion, and it refused to wither away. And to complicate this picture of worldly success there was the puzzling novelty of its intellectual position. To acknowledge one God, an omnipotent creator of the universe, but to deny the Trinity, the Incarnation, and the divinity of Christ was an intelligible philosophical position made familiar by many ancient thinkers. Likewise, to profess the immortality of the soul, the existence of a future state of rewards and punishments, and the need for such good works as almsgiving as a requirement for entry into Paradise was recognizable in this same context. But what was to be made of a doctrine that denied the divinity of Christ and the fact of his crucifixion, but acknowledged his virgin birth and his special privileges as a prophet of God; that treated the Old and New Testaments as the Word of God, but gave sole authority to a volume which intermingled confusingly the teachings of both Testaments; that accepted the philosophically respectable doctrine of future rewards and punishments, but affronted philosophy by suggesting that sexual enjoyment would form the chief delight of Paradise? A religion without priest or sacrament might be intelligible; but these characteristics of natural religion were associated with a holy Book, generally held by the few Westerners who knew it to be full of absurdities, and a divinely appointed Prophet, universally held in the West to be a man of impure life and worldly stratagem.

It was only slowly that this picture of Islam formed itself in Western minds, but in the course of time all these features came to be part of the image. Those who received its imprint may be excused if they found it puzzling. It was unlike anything else in their experience. There were times when it seemed plausible to write off the whole scheme as the fantastical product of an evil imagination. No doubt this type of explanation would have gained wide currency if Islam had shown permanent signs of decline. But this hope was constantly disappointed. Moreover, the Moslem system of thought had the adherence of men whom the

West learned increasingly, and sometimes extravagantly, to admire—scholars, philosophers, and scientists like Alfarabi, Avicenna, and Averroes, and chivalric heroes like Saladin. It was hard to believe in the simple-minded delusion of such men.

All these complicated considerations affected the Western reaction to Islam in the Middle Ages. But, as if these were not enough, there was another complication, scarcely recognized but adding immeasurably to the difficulties of any intellectual contact. Western Christendom and Islam not only represented two distinct systems of religion; they were societies extraordinarily unlike from almost every point of view. For the greater part of the Middle Ages and over most of its area, the West formed a society primarily agrarian, feudal, and monastic, at a time when the strength of Islam lay in its great cities, wealthy courts, and long lines of communication. To Western ideals essentially celibate, sacerdotal, and hierarchical, Islam opposed the outlook of a laity frankly indulgent and sensual, in principle egalitarian, enjoying a remarkable freedom of speculation, with no priests and no monasteries built into the basic structure of society as they were in the West. The development of two societies based on such contrary principles and opportunities was naturally wholly dissimilar: the West struggled through a long period of relative stagnation to achieve in the later Middle Ages a social and economic momentum which continued for centuries; Islam achieved power, wealth, and maturity almost at a bound, and never again equaled the fecundity of its earliest achievements. It continued its tradition of military success when it had lost every other symptom of its early vitality; and this early vitality, while it lasted, had no equal in the medieval West. Within four hundred years of its foundation, Islam had run through phases of intellectual growth which the West achieved only in the course of a much longer development. So much has been lost that it is impossible to speak with any exactness, but it is certain that the Islamic countries produced a greater bulk and variety of learned and scientific works in the ninth, tenth, and eleventh centuries than medieval Christendom produced in any similar length of time.[4]

The great difference between the Latin and Moslem worlds is the difference between slow growth on the one hand and precocious maturity on the other. The chief reason for this lay in the difference between their ways of life. But besides the difference in social foundation, there was also an almost complete diversity of intellectual heritage. When the ancient world fell apart into its separate parts, Islam became the chief inheritor of the science and philosophy of Greece, while the barbarian West was left with the literature of Rome. The dramatic contrast has been brought out in a remarkable paper by Dr. Richard Walzer, who has shown how Greek thought was taken over without a break from the schools of the Hellenic world into the courts and schools of Islam, and adapted to the not very exacting requirements of the Moslem religion.[5] It is the

[4] Some idea of the learned resources of Islam in the early twelfth century may be obtained from A. J. Arberry, *A Twelfth-Century Reading List: A Chapter in Arab Bibliography,* 1951.

[5] R. Walzer, "Arabic Transmission of Greek Thought to Medieval Europe," *Bulletin of the John Rylands Library,* Manchester, XXIX, 1945–46, 160–83.

most astonishing event in the history of thought, just as the rise of Islam as a political force is the most astonishing fact in the history of institutions. Islam luxuriated in abundance, while the West was left with the Church Fathers, the classical and postclassical poets, the Latin schoolmasters —works of impressive solidity but not, at least in the early Middle Ages, wildly exciting. A comparison of the literary catalogues of the West with the lists of books available to Moslem scholars makes a painful impression on a Western mind, and the contrast came as a bombshell to the Latin scholars of the twelfth century, who first had their eyes opened to the difference.

In the early period with which I am chiefly concerned in this chapter, two figures stand out as embodiments of the two cultures. They are almost exact contemporaries: in the West, Gerbert, who was born in about 940 and died as Pope in 1003; in the East, Avicenna, who was born in 980 and died in 1037. They were both men of affairs, who occupied high positions in their societies; both men of passionate intellectual curiosity; and, except for their great talents, not noticeably superior to their contemporaries in morals or practical ideals. But there the similarity ends. The courts Gerbert knew were those of Hugh Capet and Otto III, rulers living from hand to mouth, with ideas of splendor rudely contrasting with their practical impotence. The schools he knew were those of monasteries and cathedrals, certainly small and ill-equipped with books. And the books he took most pride in knowing were those that formed the slender stock of Greek science which the scholars of the last days of ancient Rome were able to hand on to their successors: Porphyry's *Introduction* to Aristotle's logic and Boethius' translations and summaries of its more elementary parts, with his handbooks on arithmetic, music, geometry, and astronomy; some fragments of Greek medical knowledge. From these scanty sources Gerbert composed his own jejune works—a chart showing the various branches of rhetoric, a textbook of arithmetic, a small specimen of dialectic; and on these foundations he built a model of the planetary system, an abacus, and a complicated clock.[6] It is a meager harvest, redeemed from insignificance by the great efforts that were necessary to raise it and the considerable advance it marked on any previous efforts of a similar kind.

If Gerbert had been born in Bukhara instead of Aurillac, and if he had taught in Baghdad or Isfahan instead of at Rheims, he would have found himself in a society intellectually much more congenial to him than that of the West, and he would have had all the books he could desire. Avicenna was born at Bukhara about forty years later than Gerbert. He lived till 1037 and died at Isfahan.[7] In contrast to Gerbert, the priest, monk, prelate, Pope, and political intriguer among laymen powerless to fulfill his grandiose plans, Avicenna was a layman, an official, a physician, and court philosopher. By the age of sixteen he had studied (as

---

[6] For Gerbert it will be sufficient here to refer to the still unsurpassed edition of his letters by J. Havet, 1889, supplemented by the Chronicle of Richer, ed. R. Latouche, in *Les classiques de l'histoire de France au Moyen Age*, 1930–1937, II, 54–56, and A. Olleris, *Oeuvres de Gerbert*, 1867.

[7] For Avicenna's autobiography, see A. J. Arberry, *Avicenna on Theology*, 1951, and for an account of his life and work, S. M. Afnan, *Avicenna: His Life and Works*, 1958.

he tells us) Porphyry's *Introduction* and all the straightforward parts of logic, together with Euclid's Geometry,
Ptolemy's *Almagest,* a whole library of Greek medicine,
some Indian arithmetic, and the inevitable and intricate
Moslem jurisprudence. Even if we allow for some element
of exaggeration in the recollections of this youthful prodigy,
the general picture of his resources is certainly not exagger-
ated: the boy had at hand riches undreamt of at this time
in western Europe. By the time he was a young man he had
devoured the logic, natural sciences, mathematics, and
metaphysics of ancient Greece, finishing with a prolonged
and painful study of Aristotle's *Metaphysics*. And all this
was not an isolated study, but an integral part of a tradition
of Moslem science already two hundred years old. Avicenna
has left us a description of the library of the Sultan of
Bukhara. It was contained in many rooms, each piled with
chests of books and each devoted to a single subject—language and poetry, law, logic, medicine, and so on—with a
catalogue from which it was possible to get a general view
of the ancient writers on each science. There was nothing
similar to this—certainly no layman had anything approaching it—in the West till the end of the Middle Ages.

There is no need to pursue the contrast any further.
Avicenna's own works were in bulk and importance a
product worthy of the mine from which they were dug.
They were composed in the midst of a busy and unsettled
life, as Avicenna moved about in the courts of present-day
Persia and the Soviet provinces of Turkmenistan and
Uzbekistan. We shall meet these works later in the West.

They were one of the agents in the breaking down of the intellectual barriers between Islam and Christendom, when the works of Gerbert were forgotten.

This contrast stands at the very beginning of our subject. Let us now look to the end.

I end this survey with the end of the Middle Ages. The problem loses much of its interest and complexity after this period. This may seem surprising. To judge only from the map, Islam pressed more menacingly on western Europe in 1600 than it had done eight hundred years earlier. It had obliterated Byzantium; it stood on the frontier of Germany and all along the southern shores of the Mediterranean. But the main problems with which we are concerned had been, if not solved, at least shelved. In the vastly extended world picture of the seventeenth and eighteenth centuries, the existence of Islam was no longer the challenge to the West that it had seemed to be in the Middle Ages. The divisions of Christendom blurring the contrast with the outside world, the recognition of other non-Christian systems besides that of Islam, the growing wealth of Europe, the slow decline of the great Turkish Empire, the rise of a more secular outlook on the world, and the discovery of the New World, were all factors which combined to make Islam seem less and less formidable, until Gibbon could recline in the pleasing spectacle of European pre-eminence and declare that "the reign of independent Barbarism is now contracted to a narrow span; and the remnant of Calmucks or Uzbucks, whose force may be almost numbered, cannot seriously excite the apprehensions of the great re-

public of Europe." [8] For Gibbon the menace of Islam was
only a memory that might serve to warn Europe not to
indulge *too* freely in the prospect of endless security: "This
apparent security should not tempt us to forget that new
enemies, and unknown dangers, may *possibly* arise from
some obscure people, scarcely visible in the map of the
world. The Arabs or Saracens, who spread their conquests
from India to Spain, had languished in poverty and contempt, till Mahomet breathed into those savage bodies the
soul of enthusiasm." Despite this cautionary word we can
sense that Mahomet and his savage enthusiasts have been
safely relegated to the realm of legend with Tamburlaine
and the great conquerors of antiquity. Intellectually and
materially Europe felt safe.

The Middle Ages were the Golden Age of the Islamic
problem. During the centuries between about 650 and 1570
it rose and fell. But the rise and fall were not a simple
or a single movement. Nothing is more striking on a close
observation than the extremely slow penetration of Islam as
an intellectually identifiable fact in Western minds, followed after the year 1100 or thereabouts by a bewildering
rapidity of shifting attitudes, in which the Islamic problem
constantly took on new forms, partly in response to changes
in the practical relations between East and West, but even
more profoundly as a result of the changing interests and
equipment of thought in Europe itself.

For the purposes of this study I have distinguished three

[8] Gibbon, *History of the Decline and Fall of the Roman Empire,*
chapter xxxviii, "General Observations on the Fall of the Roman Empire
in the West."

phases and I have attempted a brief characterization of each in the title of each chapter. We are concerned first with what I have called the age of ignorance, and ignorance may appear to be treated with too much indulgence in being accorded even what remains of this chapter. But ignorance is itself a phenomenon of great complexity. Theologians have identified twenty-four different kinds of ignorance, and we might learn something from their elaborate and ingenious distinctions; but for our present purpose we may adopt a cruder classification, and content ourselves with two varieties. I shall call them the ignorance of a confined space and the ignorance of a triumphant imagination. The first was the predominant note of the Western attitude to Islam during the four centuries after A.D. 700; the second was the creation and characteristic attitude of the forty years from 1100 to about 1140. The first of these attitudes was closely connected with Biblical exegesis, the second with the imaginative creativity of the early twelfth century. In what remains of this chapter I shall examine the chief features of these attitudes and indicate their influence on the future.

II

To turn first to the ignorance of confined space. This is the kind of ignorance of a man in prison who hear rumors of outside events and attempts to give a shape to what he hears, with the help of his preconceived ideas. Western writers before 1100 were in this situation with regard to Islam. They knew virtually nothing of Islam as a religion. For them Islam was only one of a large number of enemies threatening Christendom from every direction, and they

had no interest in distinguishing the primitive idolatries of
Northmen, Slavs, and Magyars from the monotheism of
Islam, or the Manichaean heresy from that of Mahomet.
There is no sign that anyone in northern Europe had even
heard the name of Mahomet. Yet, despite their ignorance,
Latin writers were not left entirely without a clue to the
place of the Saracens in the general scheme of world history.
This clue was provided by the Bible.

   In the interpreting of present events it is clear that the
Bible can do two things. It can explain their origins or
their ultimate fate, their beginning or their end. In the main
scholarly tradition of the period from 700 to 1100 the role
of the Bible was confined to its use in discovering the
distant origins of the Saracens in Old Testament history,
and establishing their general relationship to the peoples
and religions of the world. For a few scholars, however, it
pointed to the future and displayed the place of the Saracens
in the impending end of all things. Searching the Scriptures
was not in the end very helpful in explaining the phenomenon of Islam, but a short consideration of this method of
inquiry is necessary if we are to understand the manner in
which Islam first became a familiar object to Western
minds: whether right or wrong it had a great influence on
later thought and action. Nor is this surprising. The Bible
was the one effective intellectual tool of the early Middle
Ages. It would have been absurd to ignore its statements
about either the past or the future, however puzzling these
might be; and it was an essential part of the education of
the Western world to learn, often by bitter experience, what
the Bible could and could not tell men about the world they

lived in. Biblical scholars could make no more important contribution to the future than in examining this problem.

Bede

We must start with Bede, the great Biblical master of the early Middle Ages.[9] He commanded the whole Biblical scholarship of his day, and what he wrote was the foundation of this branch of learning until the twelfth century. Moreover, the Saracens first became a matter of European concern during his lifetime, and before he died they had reached the limit of their westward expansion. It is therefore somewhat surprising to note that the Saracens of his day made no specially forcible impact on him. He saw them as unbelievers of not more than ordinary ferocity, and in his *History* (where of course they were not part of his main theme) a single sentence sufficed to relate their ravages and the due reward for them which they received at Poitiers. In his Biblical commentaries Bede was rather more expansive: here he had something of interest to relate. At various points he explains that the Saracens were descendants of Hagar, the Egyptian wife of Abraham, of whom we read in the Book of Genesis.[10] You will remember that

[9] Most of Bede's references to the Saracens have been collected by C. Plummer in his edition of the *Historia Ecclesiastica*, 1896, II, 339. In addition, see M. L. W. Laistner, *Bedae Venerabilis Expositio Actuum Apostolorum et Retractatio*, 1939, pp. 34, 149, 152, 157.

[10] The identification had been made by Eusebius at the beginning of the fourth century, and even earlier by Josephus. Bede's immediate source was Isidore of Seville; but it is noticeable that Isidore said nothing about the Saracens in his comments on Genesis, chapters viii and xvii (*P.L.* LXXXIII, 242, 248–49): here he confined himself to the traditional identification of the children of Hagar with the Jews.

Abraham had two wives, Sarah and Hagar, whose sons were respectively Isaac and Ishmael. In Christian symbolism Isaac, the son of the freewoman, prefigured Christ, and his descendants the Church. Similarly Ishmael and his descendants represented the Jews. That was the allegorical meaning of the events described in Genesis. But *literally* the actual descendants of Ishmael were held to be the Saracens. There was much in the known facts about their life to justify this identification. Ishmael had been driven into the desert: *they* came from the desert. Ishmael was a wild man whose hand was against every man's: could any better description of the Saracens be found than this? Ishmael was outside the Covenant: so were the Saracens. There were several other ways in which the character of the Saracens could be understood in the light of this identification with the children of Ishmael, and Bede was not the first to make it. But it was he who introduced it into the medieval tradition of Biblical exegesis, and after his day it was a commonplace of Western scholarship. It helped to soften the harsh dichotomy between Christendom and those unpredictable enemies. It gave them a niche in Christian history.

The problems raised by this identification gave a certain amount of trouble to Bede and his successors, but they were problems of a cloistered learning. Why, for example, were these people called *Saracens* if they were descended not from *Sarah* but from *Hagar*? This is the kind of question that scholarly writers liked to investigate, and it is unnecessary for us to follow them in their abstruse speculations.[11]

[11] Greek writers attributed the name to a pun: τῆς Σαρρᾶς κενούς = *a Sarra vacuos,* following the words of Hagar "Sarra vacuam me dimisit"

They added nothing to the main picture of events. What surprises us most in Bede and his Carolingian successors is the lack of rancor in their account of the Saracens. They were ravaging or threatening half Europe, but they aroused less bitter hostility than they did later. There were no doubt many reasons for this. The writers of northern Europe were fairly remote from the Saracens and the danger they presented. There were nearer enemies, many of them not on the frontiers of Christendom but at the walls of the monastery; and in the cosmic struggle of Good and Evil the Saracens had a relatively humble role. Having identified them and placed them in their Old Testament context the Carolingian scholars had done all they could. They could turn to the literary problems, in which they showed an inordinate interest. They were happier discussing the spelling of "Sarah," whether it should have one or two *r*'s, than in discussing the nature of the Saracens.[12] Of course they were much better equipped for discussing the first than for the second, and they turned to such problems with enthusiasm.

But though this might be the prevailing outlook of

(see John of Damascus, *De Haerisibus, P.G.* XCIV, 763). This interpretation, however, was not open to the Latins, who had to seek another explanation. The possible explanations are given by Isidore: either the Saracens claimed (wrongly) to be descended from Sarah, *a Sarra geniti,* or they were so called from their Syrian origin, *quasi Syrigenae* (*P.L.* LXXXII, 329, 333).

[12] There is a long discussion of this point in the Commentary on Genesis of Angelomus of Luxeuil, an author of the mid-ninth century who felt himself to be in the direct tradition of Alcuin and to be maintaining the highest standards of Carolingian scholarship (*P.L.* CXV, 179ff.).

scholars in northern Europe, there were others who rejected this attitude of learned detachment and who turned from Biblical history to Biblical prophecy in their attempt to understand Islam. The men who did this lived in Spain and wrote in the middle of the ninth century.

Spanish Apocalyptic Thought

It is a remarkable fact that every single important novelty we shall touch upon can be traced back in its origin to Spain. Even Bede's identification of the Saracens with the sons of Hagar came immediately from Isidore of Seville. This is the pattern throughout the Middle Ages. The large constructions, the great systems and elaborations of ideas, were produced elsewhere, but the seminal ideas, whether apocalyptic or scientific or synoptic, came out of Spain. Spain was the country which suffered most from, and therefore thought most about, Islam. We generally imagine Spanish thought about Islam to have been violent, uncompromising, and fanatical. But this image, which has impressed itself as normal, represents only a short phase, or rather two short phases, almost at the beginning and at the very end of the Middle Ages. Between these two extremes, between the ninth and the sixteenth centuries, there is a long period in which Spanish influence was very varied but almost wholly rational and beneficent. And even at the beginning and end, when Spain was the spearhead of violence and intolerance, the reaction is thoroughly intelligible in the circumstances of the time.

This can be illustrated at once by returning to Spain in the middle of the ninth century. The situation of the Chris-

tian community in the greater part of Spain at this time was
identical with that of many Christian communities throughout the Islamic world.[13] In accordance with the teaching
of the Koran they were given protection on condition of
paying tribute. They had their own bishops, priests,
churches, and monasteries, and many of their number were
in responsible positions in the service of the Emirs of
Cordova. So far, so good. But it was also laid down in the
Koran that the Christians, though tolerated and protected,
should nevertheless be "brought low." [14] In effect this meant
no publicity of worship, no ringing of bells, no proces-
sions, and of course no blaspheming of the Prophet or Book
of Islam. Further, they were in a position of extreme isolation from the rest of Christendom, and of ignorance of the
sources of Latin learning, both secular and ecclesiastical.
The relations between Cordova and northern Europe do not
yet appear to have been rejuvenated by the slave trade,
which began to be brisk with the German conquests of
Slavonic lands in the tenth century. The only account we
have of a journey of Northern monks to Cordova at this
time records that there had been no caravan from the
frontier town of Saragossa to Cordova for eight years.[15]

[13] For the general situation, see E. Lévi-Provençal, *Histoire de l'Espagne
musulmane,* 2nd ed., 1950, I, 225–39, and for a lively but one-sided account
of the events of this period, R. Dozy, *Histoire des Musulmans d'Espagne,*
new ed., 1932, I, 317ff.

[14] Koran, ix (ed. G. Sale, p. 137).

[15] Two monks of S. Germain-des-Prés in search of the relics of St.
Vincent in 858 finally found their way to Cordova and returned to
northern Europe with the bodies of three of the recently martyred Spanish
saints. They have left a valuable account of their travels, and it was
through them that knowledge of the Spanish movement reached the
North. The Emperor Charles the Bald took an interest in the affair and
later sent for more information. On all this, see (besides the general

This was in 858, at the height of the events I am about to relate. As for the profound isolation of the Cordovan Christians, it cannot be more clearly illustrated than by the experience of their leading scholar, who visited Navarre in 848 and brought back books at that time unobtainable in Cordova, among them, Augustine's *City of God*, Virgil, Horace, Juvenal.[16] If such works as these were unobtainable, what hold can the Christians of Cordova have had on the civilization of Rome?

In the midst of a brilliant and flourishing civilization, with its Arabic literature and its genial virtues, it was inevitable that the temper of the Christian population should become relaxed. This had happened in the end wherever Islam was established, and it was happening in Spain:

The Christians love to read the poems and romances of the Arabs; they study the Arab theologians and philosophers, not to refute them but to form a correct and elegant Arabic. Where is the layman who now reads the Latin commentaries on the Holy Scriptures, or who studies the Gospels, prophets or apostles? Alas! all talented young Christians read and study with enthusiasm the Arab books; they gather immense libraries at great expense; they despise the Christian literature as unworthy of attention. They have forgotten their language. For every one who can write a letter in Latin to a friend, there are a thousand who can express themselves in Arabic with elegance, and write better poems in this language than the Arabs themselves.[17]

---

works already mentioned) B. de Gaiffier, "Les notices hispaniques dans le Martyrologe d'Usuard," *Analecta Bollandiana,* LV, 1937, 268–83.

[16] Paul Alvarus, *Vita Eulogii,* cap. iii (*P.L.* CXV, 712).

[17] Paul Alvarus, *Indiculus Luminosus, P.L.* CXXI, 555–56, quoted in Dozy, *Musulmans d'Espagne,* I, 317.

The situation was a familiar one in Islam. The West was to have plenty of opportunity to observe the corrosive effect of Moslem virtues when placed side by side with Christian virtues, and there was probably no way short of conquest or conversion by which the process could be arrested. But for a few years between 850 and 860, the sense of being gradually suffocated provoked a reaction among a handful of Christians, and led to protests—not so much against Islam as against the complacency of their fellow Christians—and to martyrdoms.

The men who led this reaction were a priest, Eulogius, and a layman, Paul Alvarus.[18] Eulogius became titular bishop of Toledo, and died a martyr in 859. He wrote an account of the movement from which we derive most of our information about it. Paul Alvarus wrote a polemical work, the *Indiculus Luminosus,* attacking those Christians —and they were the majority—who counseled moderation. He also wrote the *Life of Eulogius,* and the ideas of the two men are so similar that they may for our purposes be treated as one. Briefly, they were both inspired by the idea that the rule of Islam was a preparation for the final appearance of Antichrist, and they found in the Bible the evidences they needed. Such evidences were not difficult to find. If they had been skeptical men, the very ease with which the search was successful might have warned them that it was futile. But they were not skeptical men, and they have had a long line of successors who were not skeptical men. When Alvarus

[18] For their works, see *P.L.* CXV, 705–870; CXXI, 397–566; and for recent studies and editions see C. M. Sage, *Paul Albar of Cordoba: Studies on his Life and Writings,* 1943, and J. Madoz, *Epistolario de Alvaro de Cordoba,* 1947.

read the following words in the Book of Daniel, he knew
what they meant, and he saw how they illuminated the
situation of his own day:[19]

*The fourth beast shall be the fourth kingdom upon earth, which
shall be different from all kingdoms, and shall devour the whole
earth, and shall tread it down, and break it in pieces.*

In traditional Christian thought this was the Roman Empire, the fourth world power following the Empires of the
Assyrians, Persians, and Greeks.[20]

*And the ten horns of the kingdom are the ten kings that shall
arise.*

Here were the barbarian invaders who had destroyed the
Empire.

*And another shall arise after them and he shall be different
from the first; and he shall subdue three kings.*

Here were the followers of Mahomet with their vast empire
triumphing over Greeks, Franks, and Goths.

*And he shall speak great words against the Most High, and
shall wear out the saints of the Most High, and think to change
times and laws.*

Did not Mahomet, the Moslem calendar, and the Koran do
these very things?

*and they shall be given into his hand for three and a half periods
of time.*

[19] In the following paragraph I have summarized the comments on
Daniel vii, 23–25, in the *Indiculus Luminosus*, *P.L.* CXXI, 535–36.
[20] For the theory of the four empires in early Christian literature, see
J. W. Swain in *Classical Philology*, XXXV, 1940, 18–21.

Here was the crux of the matter. I have taken a liberty with
the text,[21] but it was a liberty taken by our author. Paul
Alvarus interpreted this obscure phrase to mean that Islam
would flourish for three and a half periods of seventy years
each; that is, for 245 years in all. Now since he was writing
in 854, and the beginning of the Moslem era was in 622
(or, as he probably believed, 618), it is evident that the end
of the world was very close. By a curious coincidence—since
everything conspires to support a hypothesis we desire to
believe—the Emir of Cordova Abd ar-Rahman III died in
852 and he was succeeded by Mahomet I, "the man of
damnation of our time." The congruity of name with that
of the great deceiver himself might have emboldened
a more cautious scholar than Paul Alvarus to proclaim that
the end of all things was at hand.

I shall not pursue into the Books of Job and the Apocalypse the intricate calculations of these persecuted men.
Their distress of mind and the urgent duty they felt to rouse
their fellows to a sense of their danger and mission gives
dignity to a system which intellectually has nothing to
recommend it. And this is more than can be said of many
of those who have followed in their footsteps. It was not
difficult for them to find in Islam and its founder the signs
of a sinister conspiracy against Christianity. They thought
they saw in all its details—and they knew very few—that
total negation of Christianity which would mark the con-
trivances of Antichrist. They had in their possession a brief

---

[21] The Vulgate reads: "et tradentur in manu eius usque ad tempus, et
tempora, et dimidium temporis."

life of Mahomet, a product of Spanish ingenuity working on Byzantine tradition, and this taught them that he had died in the year 666 of the Era of Spain.[22] They cannot have been surprised to find that this was the number of the Beast of Revelation, who is the figure of Antichrist. Nor can they have been surprised to find that the life of Mahomet was a parody of the life of Christ.

Whatever else may be said of all this, it was the first rigidly coherent and comprehensive view of Islam, related to contemporary circumstances, to be developed in the West. It was a product of ignorance, but ignorance of a peculiarly complex kind. The men who developed this view were men writing of what they had deeply experienced, and they related their experience to the one firm foundation available to them—the Bible. They were ignorant of Islam, not because they were far removed from it like the Carolingian scholars, but for the contrary reason that they were in the middle of it. If they saw and understood little of what went on round them, and if they knew nothing of Islam as a religion, it was because they wished to know nothing. The situation of an oppressed and unpopular minority within a minority is not a suitable one for scientific inquiry into the true position of the oppressor. Significantly they preferred to know about Mahomet from the meager Latin source

[22] This life of Mahomet appears in several slightly different forms. Eulogius, *Liber Apologeticus Martyrum,* cap. 15, says that he found it in Navarre at the monastery of Leyre near Pampelona (*P.L.* CXV, 859). It was clearly a Spanish product because its symbolism depends on the use of the chronological Era of Spain, which was 38 years in advance of the normal reckoning.

which Eulogius found in Christian Navarre, rather then from the fountainhead of the Koran or the great biographical compilations of their Moslem contemporaries. They were fleeing from the embrace of Islam: it is not likely that they would turn to Islam to understand what it was they were fleeing from.

The Carolingian Tradition

Although views similar to those of Eulogius and Paul Alvarus reappear spasmodically in the West, it is surprising —considering the ease with which these views could be maintained and the evidence that could be brought in their favor—that they never gained general assent. The Carolingian contemporaries of these Spanish writers showed no inclination to follow their line of thought. Some faint knowledge of the lives of the Spanish martyrs penetrated to the North, and a knowledge of their ideas may have inspired discussions about Antichrist and the end of the world. But in discussing this theme, the Northern scholars ignored the role of the Saracens.[23]

There is one exception to this rule which may be mentioned because it illustrates the very great difference of temper between the scholars of Northern Europe and Christian Spain at this time. An exact contemporary of Eulogius

[23] The most influential of the Northern accounts of the end of the world was the *De Ortu et tempore Antichristi* of Adso, abbot of St. Benigne of Dijon. This work (ed. Sackur, *Sibyllinische Texte u. Forschungen*) set a fashion in ignoring the role of the Saracens. Two hundred years after its composition, the advisers of Richard I appealed to its teaching in order to contradict the novelties of Joachim of Fiore (see below, page 40).

and Paul Alvarus, Paschasius Radbertus, the most learned
man of his day in the North, discussed the signs of the last
days in his vast commentary on Matthew. Here he mentioned the Saracens, not to prove that they were the embodi-
ment of Antichrist, but to demonstrate the mild and
academic thesis that the existence of Islam outside the
Church did not prove that the last days were *necessarily* still
far distant.[24] On this great and awe-inspiring subject the
Carolingians were in the best tradition of medieval thought
—they counseled caution and sobriety. It was counsel easy
to give in a Northern monastery with the Saracens far
away and other evils near at hand. But we shall find that
whenever the situation became really menacing, and par-
ticularly when the menace of complacency within was
matched by the menace of danger without, the apocalyptic
interpretation of Islam had a new lease of life.

III

The relationship between Christendom and Islam
changed abruptly with the First Crusade. This event did
not bring knowledge. Quite the contrary. The first Crusaders and those who immediately followed them to Palestine
saw and understood extraordinarily little of the Eastern
scene. The early success discouraged any immediate re-

[24] *P.L.* CXX, 804ff. Matthew xxiv, 14, states that "the gospel of the
kingdom shall be preached in all the world . . . and then the end shall
come." Paschasius argues that this state of affairs has almost, if not quite,
been reached: preachers have reached the Scandinavian peoples and the
western islands, and, as for the Saracens, it cannot be said that they have
not heard the Gospel, though they have rejected it. However, even though
the Gospel may have been preached in all the world, we still cannot tell
how long an interval must elapse before the end of the world.

actions other than those of triumph and contempt. But they also made the religion and founder of Islam for the first time familiar concepts in the West. Before 1100 I have found only one mention of the name of Mahomet in medieval literature outside Spain and Southern Italy.[25] But from about the year 1120 everyone in the West had some picture of what Islam meant, and who Mahomet was. The picture was brilliantly clear, but it was not knowledge, and its details were only accidentally true. Its authors luxuriated in the ignorance of triumphant imagination.

The picture of the Prophet and nature of Islam formed in Europe during the first forty years or so of the twelfth century was born in triumph. It was pieced together in northern France, stimulated perhaps by the fireside stories of returning warriors and clerks far behind the line of battle; in schools and monasteries it was given a form congenial to Western minds. The result was a popular image of astonishing tenacity which outlived the rise and fall of many better systems.

In order to understand the tenacity of the fictions of this

[25] Ralph Glaber in his *History* (ed. M. Prou, 1886, pp. 11–12) recalls an incident in the life of Abbot Majolus of Cluny in 972. The abbot had been captured by the Saracens of La Garde–Fresnet. He dropped his Bible and one of the Saracens put his foot on it. But he was reproved by some of the milder spirits among the Saracens for this insult to the Prophets. Ralph Glaber adds that the Saracens believe that the Old Testament prophecies were fulfilled in Mahomet, and that they have genealogies tracing the descent of Mahomet from Ishmael, similar to the genealogy of Christ at the beginning of St. Matthew's Gospel. This passage is interesting, not only for its mention of Mahomet, but as the first account of the Moslem religion in northern Europe, and the first evidence of the contact between Cluny and Islam, which bore fruit in the translation of the Koran under Peter the Venerable.

period we must notice that they were formed at a moment of great imaginative development in western Europe. The romances of Charlemagne and soon those of Arthur; the Miracles of the Virgin; the wonders of Rome and the legends of Virgil; the legendary history of Britain—they are all products of approximately the same period and of precisely the same point of view as that which produced the legends of Mahomet and the fantastic descriptions of Moslem practices. There can be little doubt that at the moment of their formation these legends and fantasies were taken to represent a more or less truthful account of what they purported to describe. But as soon as they were produced they took on a literary life of their own. At the level of popular poetry, the picture of Mahomet and his Saracens changed very little from generation to generation. Like well-loved characters of fiction, they were expected to display certain characteristics, and authors faithfully reproduced them for hundreds of years. It would be hard to say when these characters came to be recognized as mere figments with which to frighten naughty children; but this was certainly not their original status.

It would not help our inquiry to analyze the productions of this time in detail. They belong less to the history of Western thought about Islam than to the history of the Western imagination. But a word is necessary about the sources on which the writers of this period drew.

So far as the life of Mahomet is concerned, Western writers had a few facts derived ultimately from Byzantine writers.[26] These facts concerned his marriage to a rich

[26] The picture of Mahomet and his followers which became current in

widow, his fits, his Christian background, and his plan of general sexual license as an instrument for the destruction of Christendom. But on this meager framework, to which no chronology could be attached, a great edifice was erected. When Latin writers first asked what kind of man Mahomet

---

northern Europe in the first half of the twelfth century can best be studied in the following accounts of Mahomet's life:

(1) Embrico of Mainz, *Vita Mahumeti* (ed. F. Hübner, *Historische Vierteljahrschrift*, N.F. XXIX, 1935, 441–90), a poem of 1142 lines in rhymed elegiac couplets. The poem is ascribed to Hildebert of Tours in some MSS, but this ascription cannot be accepted. We know, however, nothing about Embrico. He is often identified with the dean of Mainz of this name who became bishop of Augsburg in 1064 and died in 1077. But there are objections to this view which have not been dispelled by its latest defender, G. Cambier in *Latomus*, XVI, 1957, 468–79: in the first place, the panegyrical poem on the author written apparently after his death does not mention that he became a bishop; and secondly, the matter and style of the work are more consistent with a twelfth than with an eleventh century date. G. Cambier has answers to these objections, but they do not seem to me convincing. For a better suggestion, viz. Embrico, treasurer of Mainz 1090–1112, see W. Wattenbach, *Deutschlands Geschichtsquellen im Mittelalter,* ed. R. Holtzmann, I, 1948, 450. In any case the MSS are all of the twelfth century or later. Ten of the fourteen existing MSS come from the twelfth or early thirteenth century, and they sufficiently show the date at which the work was popular.

(2) Walter of Compiègne, *Otia de Machomete* (ed. R. B. C. Huygens, *Sacris Erudiri,* VIII, 1956, 286–328), a poem of 1090 lines, written between 1137 and 1155, and probably early in this period.

(3) Guibert of Nogent, *Gesta Dei per Francos,* i, 3 (*P.L.* CLVI, 679– 838). In his account of the First Crusade, completed before 1112, Guibert devoted a chapter to the life of Mahomet.

These accounts differ in detail but they represent the same state of knowledge and show the same attitude toward the subject. They are all based on oral testimony, Walter of Compiègne giving an elaborate account of the steps by which his information was derived from a converted Moslem. Except for Embrico, who is wildly wrong, they are all quite vague about the date at which Mahomet lived. They are all embellished with extravagant detail of more or less the same kind, and only in the faintest degree historical.

was and why he was successful, they replied that he was a
magician who had destroyed the Church in Africa and the
East by magic and cunning, and had clinched his success by
authorizing promiscuity. Some of the details—such as the
role of the white bull which terrorized the population and
finally carried the new Law between its horns, or the
account of the suspension of Mahomet's tomb in mid-air by
means of magnets—belong to folklore; others—such as
Mahomet's death and destruction by pigs during one of his
fits—are a hateful elaboration of some details in the Byzantine tradition. Some details may have a tenuous connection
with the vast mass of legends about the Prophet current in
Islam; others are pure invention.[27] The spirit of this
literature is well expressed by the most learned of the
authors responsible for it. Guibert of Nogent's brief account
of Mahomet is one of the earliest biographies of the Prophet
produced in the West outside Spain. He had more scruples
about his sources than many of his contemporaries in
northern France, and he frankly admitted that he had no
written source for his account of Mahomet.[28] What he gives
is the *plebeia opinio*. Whether it is true or false he cannot
say; but this he can say: "it is safe to speak evil of one whose
malignity exceeds whatever ill can be spoken." In a variety
of forms, whether for praise or blame, this rule inspired a

[27] Mr. R. W. Hunt has drawn my attention to the first of a series of
articles by G. Cambier, "Les sources de la Vita Mahumeti d'Embricon
de Mayence," *Latomus,* XX, 1961, 100–15, in which the echoes of Byzantine, Arabic, and classical legends in this work are discussed.

[28] He was unaware of the Prophet's real name and calls him Mathomus,
and he thought he must belong to a date not far removed from his own
time.

great deal of writing in the first half of the twelfth century. The following of it gave a large freedom to the imagination.

The same freedom formed the picture of the Moslem faith, which became current in all the epic poems of the West, from the *Song of Roland* onwards.[29] In these works the Saracens were uniformly idolaters. In the *Song of Roland* they worshiped three gods, Tervagan, Mahomet, and Apollo; but later, by a natural process of development, they had many more. Over thirty of their gods have been counted in this literature: they form a picturesque team, including Lucifer, Jupiter, Diana, Plato, and Antichrist. But this is only the abundance of popular fantasy: very soon anyone who cared to know about Islam knew that it was the most rigidly monotheistic of religions. At first, however, it is likely that the Latins, who had no experience of religions other than their own, could only imagine error taking the form of extravagance along familiar lines. If Christians worshiped a Trinity, so (they imagined) must Moslems, but an absurd one; if Christians worshiped their Founder, so (they imagined) must Moslems, but with depraved rites suitable to a depraved man and a depraved people.

Men inevitably shape the world they do not know in the likeness of the world they do know. Nowhere is this more clear than in the early Latin literature about Islam. In this chapter we have examined interpretations of Islam based on different kinds of ignorance. It is not pleasant, and it

[29] The character of the Saracens in this literature has been analyzed by W. W. Comfort, "The Saracens in the French Epic," *Publications of the Modern Language Association of America,* LV, 1940, 628–59.

may be thought profitless, to dwell on ignorance in whatever form. But these attempts at interpreting Islam had a profound influence on future thought. They gave Islam a place in three of the great traditions of European thought and sentiment, those of Biblical history, apocalyptic vision, and popular imagination. It is impossible not to feel a strong sympathy with the sobriety with which Bede and the Carolingian scholars used their exiguous sources. And the sufferings of the Spaniards gives a certain dignity to their wilder efforts. For the imaginative reconstructions of the early twelfth century it is difficult to say much that is favorable. The wanton errors of successful strength are less excusable than the errors forced out of ignorance by suffering. But the fantasies of the early twelfth century were, as we shall see, closely related to the beginning of a new and more critical spirit of inquiry. And it is this spirit, certainly more congenial to our modern ways of thought than those we have examined thus far, which I shall attempt to illustrate in the next chapter.

II

THE CENTURY OF REASON AND HOPE

At the end of the last chapter I said that the fantasies of the early twelfth century could to some extent be justified as a vehicle for a more critical appraisal of Islam than we have previously met with. It is certainly a striking fact that just as science and magic are in their origins indistinguishable, so imagination and observation seem to have some hidden affinity which makes the former promote the growth of the latter. Hence it is perhaps not surprising that the first accurate observations in the West about Islam as a religion were made by men who contributed largely to the imaginative literature of the period. I think at once of William of Malmesbury, whose histories display so avid an interest in marvels and magic, but who was also the first, so far as I know, to distinguish clearly between the idolatry and pagan superstitions of the Slavs and the monotheism of Islam, and to emphasize against all current popular thought that Islam held Mahomet not as God but as His prophet.[1] William wrote these words in about the year 1120, when the flood of misrepresentation on this subject was at its height. Or again, there is the very remarkable man, Petrus Alfonsi, a Spanish Jew who was converted to Christianity in 1106 and later made his home in England as physician to King Henry I. Besides being the first transmitter of Eastern legends in Latin, and the first exponent of Arabic science in the West, he has also left the earliest account of Mahomet and his religion which has any objective value.[2] Although hostile, he at least presents Islam as a possible choice for an uncommitted man to make. Or again, in one of the least likely of sources, in the *History of Charlemagne* of the Pseudo-Turpin, which probably belongs to a period shortly before 1150, there is a mixture which is characteristic of the time.[3] In this work there is all the usual detail about the

---

[1] *Gesta Regum,* ed. W. Stubbs (Rolls Series), p. 230, where William remarks that the Wends and the Letts are almost the only pagans still left in the world, *nam Saraceni et Turchi Deum Creatorem colunt, Mahomet non Deum sed eius prophetam aestimantes.*

[2] The account and criticism of the Moslem faith in Petrus Alfonsi's Dialogue of a Christian and a Jew (*P.L.* CLVII, 535–672) is by far the best informed and most rational statement of the case in the twelfth century, and one of the best in the whole Middle Ages. But the circumstances of the author's life were so unusual that, though his work was fairly well known and quoted in the Middle Ages, especially in England, it did not exercise any influence on the general development of the controversy.

[3] There is great uncertainty about both the date and place of composition of the Ps-Turpin, but it can scarcely be later than 1150 and it probably comes from France—most likely, in my view, from Vienne. But on this subject there is no agreement. See the editions of H. M. Smyser, 1937, and W. M. Whitehill, *Liber Sancti Jacobi: Codex Calixtinus,* 1944; and the study by P. David, *Le Ps-Turpin* (Etudes sur le livre de S. Jacques, III), 1948.

idolatrous Saracens with which the romances of Charlemagne abound; but in the middle of it there is a theological
debate between Roland and the Saracen giant Ferracutus,
which shows a good grasp of the main points at issue between Christians and Moslems, and recognizes the strength
of the Moslem insistence on the unity of God. This may
of course be an interpolation; but if so it is a very early one,
and its presence in this romantic work of fiction illustrates
the way in which the two streams of fantasy and observation
could go happily side by side.

A similar appreciation of Moslem beliefs is found in
another source of about the same date. Otto of Freising, in
a part of his Chronicle written between 1143 and 1146,
criticized the current account of the martyrdom of Thiemo,
Archbishop of Salzburg in 1101.[4] The archbishop was reported to have been martyred because he destroyed the
Moslem idols in Cairo; but, Otto observed, this was highly
improbable because "it is known that the whole body of
Saracens worship one God and receive the Old Testament
law and the rite of circumcision. Nor do they attack Christ
or the Apostles. In this one thing alone they are far from
salvation—in denying that Jesus Christ is God or the Son
of God, and in venerating the seducer Mahomet as a great
prophet of the supreme God." By the middle of the twelfth
century, therefore, rational views of the nature of Islam
were beginning to be fairly widespread, since we can find
them casually and independently expressed by authors in
England, France, Germany, and Spain.

[4] *Chronicon,* ed. A. Hofmeister (Scriptores rerum Germanicarum in
usum scholarum), 1912, p. 317.

It often happens that the first step in a new direction, though long delayed, is taken in the end with surprising ease, but the second and third steps come up against unexpected difficulties. So it was in this case. A habit of independent inquiry became established in western Europe in the early twelfth century, and showed itself in these traces of candid appraisal of Islam. But then there was a check. It was one thing to base a reasonable judgment on facts which lay ready at hand; it was quite another to seek new information for its own sake or for the sake of some future synthesis. It is very clear to us that when matters had been brought to the point at which we have seen them in the authors I have quoted, the next step must be to obtain authoritative texts for enlarging the gap in the curtain. It must always be a matter for honorable mention in the history of Cluny that this step was in fact taken on the initiative of the Abbot of Cluny, Peter the Venerable, with remarkable promptitude. The translation of the Koran undertaken at his expense by the English scholar Robert of Ketton, and completed in July 1143, is a landmark in Islamic studies.[5] With this translation, the West had for the first time an instrument for the serious study of Islam. Its appearance brought the first short period of objective appraisal to a fitting end. But it is an end rather than a beginning. The serious study of Islam was not an object

---

[5] The epoch-making study on this subject is by Mlle. M. T. d'Alverny, "Deux traductions latines du Coran au Moyen Age," *Archives d'histoire doctrinale et littéraire du Moyen Age*, XVI, 1948, 69–131. All recent work stems from this article. For a review of the results, see J. Kritzeck, "Robert of Ketton's Translation of the Qu'an," *Islamic Quarterly*, II, 1955, 309–12.

that commended itself to the contemporaries or immediate successors of Peter the Venerable.

It is not difficult to understand why this should have been so. In the second half of the twelfth century, Europe was riddled with heresies at home, and abroad the situation with regard to Islam took a decided turn for the worse. By the end of the century the high expectations of the First Crusade had been obliterated by a long succession of military reverses. These circumstances did not provide a hopeful background for the study of Islam.

Peter the Venerable had been conscious that his work of promoting a translation of the Koran and investigating the religious tenets of Islam was not likely to meet with approval. He tried to enlist the support of Bernard of Clairvaux, and failed. He tried to justify his initiative in the context of the long-term interests of Christendom, but he had little response. Like his great Greek predecessor John of Damascus, whose work was coming to be known in the West at this time, he saw Islam as a Christian heresy, the last and greatest of the heresies, and the only one that had not been answered. Hence, in a time so full of heresies, it was (he claimed) essential that this "sink of all heresies" should be answered, if not because of its immediate danger, at least because of its ultimate threat:

If this work seem superfluous, since the enemy is not vulnerable to such weapons as these, I answer that in the Republic of the great King some things are for defense, others for decoration, and some for both. Solomon the Peaceful made arms for defense, which were not necessary in his own time. David made ornaments for the Temple, though there was no means of using them in his day. . . . So it is with this work. If the Moslems cannot be converted by it, at least it is right for the learned to support the weaker brethren in the Church, who are so easily scandalized by small things.[6]

This was Abbot Peter's excuse to his fellow Christians. He was forging weapons against heresy. To a man who considered the ravages of Manichaeism in the Western Church, the idea that the Islamic heresy might make its way in the Church was not as far-fetched as it now appears. But in fact the heresy of Mahomet—if it was a heresy— never made the slightest appeal in Europe. In the border-lands where the two religions met there were always some conversions in both directions, but never enough to inspire a sense of danger to the orthodoxy of Latin Christendom. Hence the Abbot of Cluny's suggestion that Islam required serious study in order to support the weaker brethren in the Church fell flat. If Islam was to be studied at all, it would have to be for other reasons than this.

Equally his hope that he might convert the Moslems by exposing the weaknesses of the Koran was vain, for his exposure remained buried in the obscurity of the Latin language. Islam never heard the charitable voice of the abbot of Cluny explaining, "I attack you, not as some of us often do by arms, but by words; not by force, but by reason; not in hatred, but in love. I love you; loving you, I write to you; writing to you, I invite you to salvation." [7]

Attempts to give a new direction to the discussion of problems of real difficulty never succeed unless they are

[6] *P.L.* CLXXXIX, 651–52.
[7] *P.L.* CLXXXIX, 674.

helped forward by events. The effort to place Islam in a
more generously conceived intellectual framework languished after the time of Peter the Venerable, because there
were many more pressing dangers than those to which he
drew attention. The danger which impressed most Western
observers of Islam in the late twelfth century was military,
and the simple answer to it was an increased military effort.
There were many eloquent exponents of this point of view.
The most impressive among them was Abbot Joachim of
Fiore. Joachim was not a very sensible man, but he was one
of the few genuinely prophetic figures of the Middle Ages,
who claimed with some authority to see below the surface
of events to their inner meaning. When King Richard I
was on his way to the Holy Land in 1191 he met Joachim at
Messina, and Joachim outlined to him a view of history
which brought the apocalyptic visions of the ninth century
Spanish martyrs up to date.[8] For him, as for them, the end

[8] A full account of the interview between Joachim and Richard I has
been preserved by an eye-witness, the great English historian Roger of
Howden. The authenticity of his account has long been a subject of
controversy, partly because biographers of Joachim were unwilling to
believe that he held the views here ascribed to him, and partly because
there are two widely differing accounts of the meeting. The first of these
objections has been met by the discovery and publication of the *Liber
Figurarum:* this exactly coincides with the views attributed to Joachim by
the English writer, and has been shown to portray correctly the main
lines of Joachim's thought. (See especially M. E. Reeves, "The *Liber
Figurarum* of Joachim of Fiore," *Medieval and Renaissance Studies,* II,
1950, 57–81). The second objection has been met by the discovery that
Roger of Howden was the author of *both* the accounts of the interview
with Richard I (see D. M. Stenton, "Roger of Howden and *Benedict,*"
English Historical Review, LXVIII, 1953, 574–82). As soon as this has
been pointed out, it is clear that Roger of Howden later altered his
original and contemporary account of the meeting to make it conform to
later events. For the original account, see *Gesta regis Henrici secundi*

of the world was at hand, and for him also the chief instruments of Antichrist were the Saracens. On the two flanks of Christendom, in Spain and the Holy Land, he saw the strength of Islam renewed under the Almohads in Spain and Saladin in Palestine. But with regard to the future, he hesitated. Like all who foretell the future, he had to feel his way with care. He seems to have assured King Richard that he would defeat Saladin, and in this he was certainly wrong. But the most interesting addition he made to the apocalyptic picture was his assurance that the final Antichrist was already alive and in Rome, and that he was destined to obtain the papal see.

Looking back we can see that this vision, disclosed to an incredulous band of Northern Crusaders, represents a very significant shift of emphasis in the expectations of the last days. In the last blows which were to undermine the foundations of Christendom, Joachim both elevated and depressed the role of the Saracens. He elevated them by making them the last three scourges of the Church before the final blow. He depressed them by making them only a preparation for a greater internal enemy of Christ at the heart of Christendom.[9]

This scheme of things in which Christendom was held in

Benedicti Abbatis, ed. W. Stubbs (Rolls Series), II, 151–55; for the revised account, *Chronica magistri Rogeri de Houdene,* ed. W. Stubbs (Rolls Series), III, 75–79.

[9] There is a pictorial representation of this sequence of events in the *Liber Figurarum* in L. Tondelli, *Il Libro delle Figure dell'abate Gioachino da Fiore,* tavola xiv. The same picture is in Corpus Christi College, Oxford, MS. 255A. I am greatly indebted to Miss Marjorie Reeves for her help on this whole subject.

a vice formed by a resurgent Islam and a faithless Pope reappears in many later medieval visions. These visions belong to the realm of popular speculation. When they come to the surface as expressions of informed opinion they sometimes have the patronage (as we shall see) of great names, but in the thirteenth century—with one surprising exception in Pope Innocent III[10]—the apocalyptic role of Islam had no influence on the main current of responsible thought.

II

The event which did more than anything else to change the whole aspect of the Islamic problem came from a very unexpected quarter. It was the appearance of the Mongols on the scene of history. The effects of this on the outlook for Western Christendom were many and various. In the first place, and from the moment of their appearance, the Mongols greatly enlarged the geographical horizon and increased many times the number of people known to exist in the world. There is no reason to think that anyone of importance in the West between Bede and Peter the Venerable saw beyond Islam. After centuries of neighborhood the picture had so far been enlarged that Peter the Venerable was able to estimate that Islam contained a third, or possibly

[10] In a Crusading appeal of April 1213, addressed to every part of Europe except Spain, Innocent III expressly identifies Mahomet with the Beast of the Apocalypse, "whose number is concluded in 666." He argues that since almost 600 years of this number have already passed (presumably since the Hegira of 622, or perhaps Mahomet's death in 632), his end is at hand (*P.L.* CCXVI, 817–22). It would be interesting to know the inspiration of this letter.

even a half, of the people of the world.[11] This was a step toward the truth. Christendom was shrinking in relation to the rest of the world, but Islam was still essentially a fringe phenomenon. By the middle of the thirteenth century, however, it was seen that this picture, like the estimate of numbers which accompanied it, was quite misleading. It was far too optimistic. There were ten, or possibly a hundred, unbelievers for every Christian. Nobody knew; and the estimate grew with each access of knowledge.

One consequence of this was to make the Crusade seem either quite impossible, or in need of a drastic reassessment of its aims and methods. For the rest of the Middle Ages the Western world was divided into one or other of these two camps: either no Crusading was called for, or very much more and better Crusading. The only thing that could have no place was the cheerful improvisation and short-sighted planning of the past.

Further, even the most fanatical supporters of the Crusade had to turn their minds to the intellectual content of the Moslem faith and its refutation, either to reduce the enemy's will to resist and possibly to enlist his help, or to brace the weakening sinews of the West by instilling a greater conviction into its military effort. Still more, of course, those who did not sympathize with the Crusade were committed to the task of comprehension and refutation.

To Western minds the number of unbelievers grew alarmingly in the course of the thirteenth century, but in

---

[11] Peter the Venerable's estimate varies: "eius lethali peste dimidius pene orbis infectus agnoscitur" (*P.L.* CLXXXIX, 650); "pene dimidia pars mundi" (*ibid.,* 656); *but* "pene tertiam humani generis partem" (*ibid.,* 652).

some ways the gains outweighed the losses. In the first place, even though most of the newcomers on the scene might be unbelievers, they were at least not Moslems; and however formidable the Mongols were militarily, intellectually they were soon seen to be negligible. Indeed, a very complex situation soon arose. The Mongols were very frightening. But from their geographical position their first enemy was almost bound to be not Christendom but Islam; and with a certain amount of management this geographical factor could, it was hoped, be turned into a major asset for the West.

At this point two other factors became evident. One of the first results of this contact between Europe and Asia was to bring out an unsuspected measure of agreement between Christianity and Islam. Of course, as we have seen, this had been realized by a few people quite early in the twelfth century. But in the circumstances of the twelfth century, the points of agreement had not been thought to be specially significant. The second great result of contact with the Mongols was to disclose the existence of large numbers of primitive Christians about whom the West had previously had no knowledge at all. In the thirteenth century facts and fictions about these people became very widely known, and they influenced the thought of the West about the outside world in a remarkable way.

The situation therefore as it developed in the course of the thirteenth century presented a bewildering number of causes both for hopes and fears of a quite new kind. And the way in which these worked out in practice will occupy us for the rest of this chapter.

Since our concern is not primarily with events but with the impact of these events on what we may briefly call the world picture of Western observers, it seems permissible to treat the situation I have just outlined in an episodic fashion and to single out a few moments at which clear mental images can be observed. I shall space out these moments along the chronological line 1221, 1254, 1268, and 1283, and by the time we get to 1283 we shall almost have reached the limits of the period of hope, if not of reason.

The Fifth Crusade

My first date is the date of the Fifth Crusade and the place is Damietta, at the mouth of the main easterly branch of the Nile. This Crusade is a comparatively neglected one because it had no practical result of any kind. But intellectually and emotionally it was important for many reasons. It was the only Crusade ever to be effectively directed by the Papacy with a papal legate ruthlessly driving it on to a great foreordained end. It was almost a turning point in European history. Then quite suddenly it was one of the greatest flops in history. But in the spring of 1221 all was hope. The legate reported the situation to his master, and on 13 March the Pope communicated the gist of this report to the Archbishop of Trier. Here is an extract from the Papal letter:

The Lord has manifestly begun to judge his cause, mindful of the injuries suffered by his people every day, and of the cries of those who call upon him. For behold, as our venerable brother Pelagius, Bishop of Albano, Legate of the Apostolic See, has informed us, King David, vulgarly called Prester John, a Catholic and god-fearing man, has entered Persia with a powerful army, has defeated the Sultan of Persia in a pitched battle, has penetrated twenty days' march into his kingdom and occupied it. He holds therein many cities and castles. His army is only ten days' march from Baghdad, a great and famous city, and special seat of the Caliph, whom the Saracens call their chief priest and bishop. The fear of these events has caused the Sultan of Aleppo, brother of the Sultans of Damascus and Cairo, to turn his arms, with which he was preparing to attack the Christian army at Damietta, against this king. Our legate, moreover, has sent messengers to the Georgians, themselves Catholic men and powerful in arms, asking and beseeching them to make war on the Saracens on their side. Whence we hope that, if our army at Damietta has the help which it hopes for this summer, it will with God's help easily occupy the land of Egypt, while the forces of the Saracens, which had been gathered from all parts to defend it, are dispersed to defend the frontiers of their land.[12]

Here, then, we have the first impact of the Mongols on the central mind in Christendom, and the earliest hopes raised by the appearance of large numbers of Christians outside the limits of the Greco-Roman world. The Pope was only reporting what most of the Crusaders were thinking and some were writing home. One of these letters home has survived, and it repeats with further details the Pope's account: "King David . . . nearly 400,000 men, including 132,000 Christian knights . . . Persia overrun . . . capture of Baghdad immediately expected." In short, the West was about to be released from the fear of Islam by a great Christian army advancing from the Far East. The

[12] This letter and the letter from Damietta mentioned below are printed by F. Zarncke, "Zur Sage von Prester Johannes," *Neues Archiv*, II, 1887, 612–14.

time had come for concerted action between the long-divided Oriental and Western Christians to crush their common enemy.

Much of this was fantasy, but not all. It is true that King David turned out to be Jenghis Khan, and that he died without having captured Baghdad, and that his Christian knights were a figment of the imagination, and that the Mongols were to send shivers down the spines of quiet men in Western monasteries for many years to come. But the main elements in the fantasy were in the end to identify themselves as historical facts with quite astonishing accuracy. Baghdad *did* ultimately fall to the Mongols, the eastern Christians if not knights were at least numerous, and the Christians of Georgia, if not reliable or Catholic, at least were real.

William of Rubroek

Before Baghdad finally fell in 1258 we come to the second of our chronological landmarks. It is a much more substantial one than the dreams of 1221. The date is 30 May 1254, and the place the now lost town of Karakorum, in present-day Mongolia, not far from the frontier of the U.S.S.R. This time and place provided the scene of the first world debate in modern history between representatives of East and West. It was a notable occasion, and the background to it requires a brief sketch. Nine years before this date the Genoese pope Innocent IV had dispatched John of Piano Carpini, an Italian Franciscan, to bring back a report on the state of the Mongols, on whose attitude toward the West so much depended. This was in 1245.

Four years later the first of Louis IX's lamentable Crusades foundered in the Nile waters that had destroyed the Crusades in 1221. In the shadow of this defeat, Louis dispatched the Flemish Franciscan, William of Rubroek, on another mission of inquiry among the Mongols.[13] He reached the Mongol capital in May 1254, and here the great Khan staged the debate to which I have referred. In this debate, four groups of people took part: William of Rubroek spoke for the Latins, and he was faced with representatives of the three religions of Asia—the Nestorian Christians, the Buddhists, and the Moslems. The debate lasted the whole day. I shall give you a brief summary of its development and then attempt to point out the lessons which could be drawn from it so far as these affected the relation of Islam and Christendom.

The first question was the order in which the debate was to be conducted. William of Rubroek was in one way in a weak position since he could only speak through an interpreter; but in another way he had an advantage, as a newcomer and the chief center of interest. Apart from the difficulty of language, he had two problems: first to make sure that he grappled with the right enemies in the right order; second to arrange that the right questions—that is, the ones on which he was on the strongest ground—were raised first. He dealt with both these problems in a masterly way. He began by making common cause with the Nestorians. This was an elementary tactical move. But it was

[13] William of Rubroek's account of his travels is printed in A. van den Wyngaert, *Sinica Franciscana*, I, 1929; see pp. 289–97 for the debate at Karakorum.

also important that it should be he and not his allies who conducted the argument, for, as he noted, the Nestorians had no idea how to prove anything. Their one notion of argument was to quote the Scriptures, and, as William rightly told them, this was useless, for "if you recite one Scripture our enemies will reply with another." He finally convinced his allies that he should be their spokesman, arguing that his linguistic weakness made this necessary: "If I am beaten you can take up the discussion: but if you are beaten, there is no chance that I shall be listened to." So he won his first point.

The next question was to decide whether to take on the Buddhists or the Moslems in the first instance. The Nestorians strongly favored an immediate attack on the Moslems; but here again they showed their dialectical simplicity. As William pointed out, the Christians and Moslems agreed on the fundamental points of the nature and existence of one God; so, as against the Buddhists, they would start as allies; but in a dispute with the Moslems the Christians would have no allies at all.

With some difficulty William got his way on this point also, and then the debate began. The Buddhists wanted to start by discussing whether the world was created and what happened to souls after death. But here the prudent William replied: "Friend, this is not the proper beginning. All things are from God. He is the fount and head of all. Therefore we should speak first about God, concerning whom you differ from us."

This question of procedure was referred to the Arbiters appointed by the Khan to conduct the debate, and they agreed that William's point was reasonable. So he got his way here also; and a large part of the day was spent in discussing the rival views of God, in which the Latins, Nestorians, and Moslems were all in agreement against the Buddhists.

You will scarcely want to hear the arguments that can be adduced in favor of monotheism on the one hand and polytheism on the other, and I need scarcely say that in William's account at least the monotheistic arguments had decidedly the better day. Nor is this unlikely. William could speak with the authority and precision of a long philosophical tradition; his enemies were tied up in complicated genealogies of Gods in heaven and Gods on earth, and they were unable to give a clear answer to the question of God's omnipotence. Finally they committed themselves to the view that no God is omnipotent, and at this William won the sweet triumph of a loud laugh from the Moslems among the spectators.

By this time the Nestorians were getting impatient. They wanted to have their bout with the Moslems, and William stood down to allow them to speak. Here a fresh triumph awaited him and his friends, for the Moslems declined to argue: "We concede," they said, "that your law is true and that the Gospel is true: we have no wish to dispute with you." And they confessed that in their prayers they prayed for a Christian death. So the dispute came to an end, Christians and Moslems joining together in common triumph over the Buddhists, and all drinking copiously.

We cannot of course guarantee that William of Rubroek has left an impartial account of this debate, but its main outlines seem reasonably trustworthy. And, what is more important, this is the account that came back to the West. What impression did it then make? What impression does it make now?

In the first place it demonstrated the dialectical superiority of the Latins. That long logical preparation through which the schools of the West had been grinding their way for a hundred years and more was at last bearing fruit. William of Rubroek knew how to argue on theological matters, and his opponents did not. The debate encouraged the view that dialectical victory could be fairly easily achieved. But it also showed that dialectic must be supported by a knowledge of languages if it was to be effective at the level of world affairs. Then again, it threw a great deal of light on the friends and enemies of Christendom: it helped to create a picture of the Nestorians as simple men without guile, inexperienced in argument, who needed to be taken by the hand and led along; of the Buddhists as men with very little to say for themselves that could not be easily answered; and of the Moslems as men near to Christianity, potential allies intellectually if not militarily.

William of Rubroek's diary of his experiences was not widely read. Indeed, to judge from the existing manuscripts, it seems to have been read only in England,[14] and it is not fanciful to connect its fairly wide diffusion in England with the one Englishman who is known to have met and discussed the affairs of the outside world with its author.

[14] There are five medieval manuscripts of the work: Corpus Christi College, Cambridge, MSS. 66, 181, and 407; British Museum Royal MS. 14.C.xiii; and Leyden Univ. MS. 104. The last, however, is a copy of C.C.C.C. 181.

That Englishman is Roger Bacon, and he brings us to the third episode in our series and to the treatises which he wrote for Pope Clement IV in the years 1266–1268.

Roger Bacon

Roger Bacon, despite his great fame, is a man whose life is very obscure. His known and published works are now voluminous, but they have not yet been fully studied, and on the question of their value there will probably never be any general agreement. He is a man who has been equally overpraised and undervalued, overpraised for what he did not do, undervalued for what he did. In displaying one small corner of his thought, I shall display a sensible man of statesmanlike views, better informed than most of his contemporaries, but sharing their hopes and fears, and working within the framework of the inherited methods of the great schools of Paris and Oxford.

His contact with Islam was primarily philosophical. He had grown to maturity at the moment when the philosophical impact of Moslem writers on Western theologians was making itself felt for the first time in a really powerful way. It would take us too far from our main theme to dwell at length on this fascinating subject, in which such a dramatic change is to be observed in comparison with the situation I described in the age of Gerbert and Avicenna. But since the possession of a common philosophical method was the great new bond between Islam and the West in the thirteenth century—we have seen how it affected the course of the debate far away at Karakorum—it is necessary to say a few words about the way in which this reversal of the earlier philosophical isolation of the West had come about.

The change was very largely the result of the work of a small body of devoted translators at work in Toledo in the third quarter of the twelfth century.[15] These men introduced the works of the great Moslem philosophers Al-Kindi, Al-Farabi, Avicenna, and others to the West, and to a great extent they put the West for the first time in possession of the tradition of the Greek philosophical and scientific thought which had been the formative influence in the first centuries of Islam. A large body of this work was accessible in Latin by the end of the twelfth century; but it was not until about the year 1230—when Roger Bacon was of an age to begin his university career—that the ideas and terminology of these writings made their way into Latin theology, necessarily the most difficult conquest in their victorious career. It would have startled the theologians of an earlier generation to see the name of Avicenna quoted beside that of Augustine; but this is what happened with astonishing rapidity, and modern scholars are still finding increasingly extensive traces of the influence of Moslem writers in thirteenth century theology. It has been known since the time of Renan's great work that Latin Averroism, so called from the last great Aristotelian among the Moslems, was an extensive and highly suspect school of thought

[15] There is an excellent summary of this activity in G. Théry, *Tolède, grande ville de la Renaissance médiévale,* 1944, in which references are given to the main works of earlier scholars. For later work, see A. Alonso in *al-Andalus,* XII, 1947, 295–338, and XXIII, 1958, 371–80; M. T. d'Alverney in *Archives d'histoire doctrinale et littéraire du Moyen Age,* XIX, 1952, 337–58, and in *Accademia nazionale dei Linzei,* XL, 1957, 71–87.

in the later thirteenth century; but more recently an earlier phase of what has been called Latin Avicennism has come to light; and it is probable that an early and orthodox phase of Averroism still awaits a full study.

It would be difficult to exaggerate the extent to which these influences changed the outlook of learned Europeans in the half century after 1230. It is as if modern economists in the tradition of Alfred Marshall and Keynes were suddenly to start using the language of Karl Marx, or liberal statesmen to express themselves in the idiom of Lenin. Let me give you one example of what it meant in practice.

It is one of the common tenets of Christian theology that the souls of the blessed will enjoy the direct vision of God in Paradise. When, therefore, the University of Paris in January 1241 found it necessary to condemn the contrary opinion and to reassert the traditional view, we can be sure that something had taken place to disturb the concord of theologians on this subject. The exact nature and extent of the disturbance has for some time been a matter for debate, and it is only recently that the probable source of the disturbance has been located in the influence of Avicenna, which had been making rapid strides in the West during the decade before 1241.[16] It was a view of Avicenna's that

[16] See P. M. de Contenson, "S. Thomas et l'Avicennisme latin," *Revue des sciences philosophique et théologique*, XLIII, 1959, 3–31. For the earlier literature on the subject it may suffice to refer to the same author's "Avicennisme latin et vision de Dieu au début du XIII siècle," *Archives d'hist. doct. et litt. du M.A.*, XXXIV, 1959, 29–97, and H. F. Dondaine, "L'objet et le médium de la vision béatifique chez des théologiens du XIII siècle," *Recherches de théologie ancienne et médiévale*, XIX, 1952, 60–130. The relevant decree of the University of Paris will be found in the *Chartularium Universitatis Parisiensis*, ed. Denifle and Chatelain, I, no. 128.

the Creator could never be known directly by any created being. This emphasis on the separation between God and Man is one of the points at which Islamic conceptions diverge most clearly from those of Christianity; but here under the patronage of Avicenna it appears to have made some progress in academic circles in the West. The new view called forth many replies; one of the weightiest was that of Thomas Aquinas, contained in a long discussion written in about the year 1250. Aquinas, as we should expect, supported the earlier, orthodox view that the souls of the blessed enjoy the direct vision of God; but in answering this Moslem-inspired error he used the language and formulae of another Moslem philosopher, Averroes. If, then, the error was that of Avicenna, the language of the defense was that of Averroes. On a central theological issue Western theologians of all shades of opinion in the mid-thirteenth century did not scruple to re-examine traditional views in the light of Islamic philosophy, or at least to restate traditional views in the language of these philosophers.

It is tempting to linger over this fascinating prospect of Christian theology being influenced in its views and language by Islamic philosophy. And this scholastic influence was only one aspect of a wider penetration. It seems now, for example, quite certain that a work translated into French and Latin from Arabic at about this time, giving an account of Mahomet's journey through the heavens, had an influence—perhaps a profound influence—on the plan of Dante's *Divine Comedy*.[17] When Dante placed the Islamic

[17] For recent summaries of the long-standing controversy about the influence of Islam on Dante's *Divine Comedy,* see E. Cerulli, "Dante e

philosophers Avicenna and Averroes, and the Islamic war-
rior Saladin, in Limbo as the only moderns among the
sages and heroes of antiquity, he was acknowledging a
debt of Christendom to Islam which went far beyond anything he could have expressed in words.[18] But this leads us
from our theme, and we must return to Roger Bacon and
see how he expressed the intellectual and geographical en-
largement of his lifetime.

In the years 1266–1268, Bacon achieved his long-cherished
ambition of being able to address directly to the Pope his
own uninhibited views on what was wrong with the state
of Christendom. He was a man with an itch for self-
expression, and he worked furiously, pouring out his ideas
in a series of works of varying lengths, but all covering more
or less the same ground—that is to say, all the ground there
was—with much repetition, unwise abuse of his contemporaries, and self-confident suggestions for the future. These
works are among the most famous—they are certainly
among the most readable—works of the Middle Ages.[19]
But it is only fairly recently that the actual manuscript sent
by Bacon, with his last-minute afterthoughts and special
signs to draw attention to important points, has come to
light, and much more recently that the final section of the

Islam," *al-Andalus*, XXI, 1956, 229–53, and G. Levi della Vida, "Nuova
luce sulle fonti islamiche della Divina Commedia," *al-Andalus*, XIV,
1949, 337–407.

[18] *Inferno*, iv, 129, 143–44.

[19] The three works of 1266–1268 in which he expounded his ideas on
the intellectual strategy of Christendom are the *Opus Maius* (ed. J. H.
Bridges, 3 vols., 1900) and the *Opus Minus* and the *Opus Tertium* (ed.
J. S. Brewer, Rolls Series, 1859).

Opus Maius, on Moral Philosophy, has been printed from this original manuscript.[20] It is from this that we can get our fullest idea of the impact of Islam on Roger Bacon.

We see that Bacon has now got, as he could scarcely have had at any earlier time, a true measure of the place of Christendom in the world: "there are few Christians; the whole breadth of the world is occupied by unbelievers, and there is no one to show them the truth." [21] If we ask why there is no one to show them the truth, the answer is partly that the aims of Christendom have been wrong, and partly that its equipment has been inadequate. Its aims have been wrong because they have been perverted by the desire for domination which frustrated the work of conversion. The wars have been unsuccessful; but even had they been successful they would have been useless: first because it would have been impossible to occupy so much territory, and second because the survivors would have been inflamed against their conquerors, dangerous to live with, and impossible to convert—as, he alleges, we can see in many parts of the Islamic world today. Preaching is therefore the only way in which Christendom can be enlarged.[22] But for this there is a lack of equipment in three respects: no one knows the necessary languages; the types of unbelief have not been studied and distinguished; and there has been no study of the arguments by which each can be refuted.

A large part of Bacon's work was taken up with preliminary sketches, suggestions, assertions, and some fully

[20] *Baconis Operis Maius Pars Septima seu Moralis Philosophia,* ed. E. Massa, 1953.

[21] *Opus Maius,* iii, 122.

[22] *Ibid.,* pp. 121–22.

worked-out arguments indicating the ways in which these deficiencies could be made good. In retrospect we can see that he was far too optimistic, and even without the advantages of hindsight the Pope may have been skeptical of Bacon's offer to teach him or anyone else Hebrew in three days.[23] But we must not exaggerate Bacon's optimism. He only means he could teach the meaning of the Hebrew words used by the Latin Fathers; and, as for his general optimism, it was shared by many contemporaries and encouraged by contemporary events.

On the teaching of languages Bacon is boringly repetitive. But in his attempt to analyze the various forms of unbelief, to discover the causes which brought about their rise and the influences which maintained them in being, he was stretching out toward the founding of a new science. It is true that his system of classification now seems extremely bizarre. He thought that all possible ways of life could be classified into six types according to their final end—pleasure, riches, honor, power, fame, or the felicity of a future life—and that nations could be classified according to their following one or other of these ends—the Saracens, pleasure; the Tartars, power; and so on. Further, that they could be classified according to the organization and tendency of their worship, whether they had one, or many, or no gods, or any or no priesthood. And then again classified with reference to the planetary influences under which they best throve.[24] In making these classifications Bacon was greatly influenced by Aristotle's *Politics:* Aristotle had classified states into six

---

[23] *Opus Tertium,* p. 65.
[24] *Moralis Philosophia,* pp. 189–92.

types with reference to their constitution and final end, so
he had good authority for his procedure, however strange
the final result might be. And we must certainly concede
that he had the right idea in attempting a general survey of
all the possible enemies of Christendom.

But such a survey would have little value unless accompanied by a program for meeting intellectually the enemies
disclosed by investigation. It is at this point that the role of
Islam in the economy of world history emerges in a quite
new way. Bacon begins by asserting that there are only two
ways in which the various sects he has analyzed can be
persuaded of the truth: either by miracles, or by philosophy.
He places no reliance on the availability of miracles. He has
already excluded war; he now excludes miracles. It follows
that only philosophy is left. But it is here precisely that
Christendom is weak. "Philosophy," he says, "is the special
province of the unbelievers: we have it all from them." [25]
This, then, is the role of the unbelievers—and he must be
thinking in the first place of the Greeks, and after them
of the Arabs—to provide Christianity with the philosophy
it needs to understand itself, so that philosophy can return
to them enriched by revelation.[26] There is thus a reciprocal
action in history between Christendom and the outside
world, each providing the other with what it lacks. Philosophy is the *preparatio evangelica* for the outside world, for
"the power of philosophy agrees with the wisdom of God;

[25] *Ibid.*, p. 195.
[26] For Bacon's assessment of the importance of philosophy to the Christian faith see especially *Metaphysica fratris Rogeris,* ed. R. Steele (Opera
hactenus inedita, I), pp. 6–7, 36–39.

it is the outline of the divine wisdom given by God to man, so that he may be raised up to the divine verities." [27]

Philosophy, of course, can only have this exalted role if it can convince unbelievers of their errors. Bacon takes the religions of the world one by one and gives examples of the kind of argument he thinks effective against them. He attempts to give arguments which will convince intelligent men and not simply the crowd, "for in every nation there are some able and industrious men capable of rational persuasion"; and he recognizes the need for arguing from a common ground, and for varying this ground with the enemy whom he is facing. He works through the various religions until he comes to Islam, which he recognizes as the most difficult case of all. Against Islam, he gives a long series of arguments capable, as he thinks, of refuting it. These are all cast in the form of syllogisms in which the premises are either taken from or suggested by Islamic writers.[28] I do not think they would be likely to win many converts, though to a Western mind they are certainly not without some force. Bacon made the mistake of drawing premises indiscriminately from the Koran and from Islamic philosophers who were not as representative of Islam as he, with the example of the Latin scholastic theologians before his eyes, imagined. They could be, and in fact largely were, jettisoned by orthodox Moslems at this very time. And he argued altogether too glibly in administering his blows, designed to reduce Islam to dust in a succession of rapid

[27] *Moralis Philosophia*, p. 196.
[28] *Ibid.*, pp. 218–23.

assaults. But we must not be too harsh in judging suggestions thrown out at the end of nearly a thousand pages of
argument and expostulation, written in haste, with no en-
couragement, at his own expense, and for the good of
Christendom. The work was a notable example of the
combination of opportunity and zeal. In its completeness
and system, its confidence in argument, and its recognition
of the philosophical strength of Islam, it marks the peak in
the coincidence of hope and reason.

Let me pause for a minute to point out the great difference between this world picture of Bacon and those of the
writers we have already discussed. The first and most important difference is that, whereas earlier thinkers had seen
Islam as a religion with only a negative role in history as a
falling away from the truth, a preparation for the final
holocaust of Antichrist, part of a downward movement,
Bacon (and he is not the only man of his time to see this)
had some conception of an upward movement toward unity
and articulateness in which Islam had an essential role to
play before it withered away. He entirely abandoned the
Bible as an instrument for understanding the role of Islam
in the world, and relied exclusively on philosophy. For his
knowledge of Islam he relied on Moslem philosophers and
the experience of travelers, and not on the meager and
casual fragments of information which characterized the
earlier writers. The philosophers and travelers were less
reliable guides than he supposed. He did not know a great
deal, and perhaps he did not know the right things, but he
tried to know, and he tried to organize his knowledge.

The Hopeful Decades

Although Bacon disappears from view after 1268, or only fitfully appears in disgrace or prison, the mood in which he wrote appeared for some time to be consistent with the facts. The reports of travelers in the East during the next twenty years maintained the same mood of optimism. For instance, William of Tripoli, a Dominican friar at Acre, wrote an account of Islam for the archdeacon of Liége in 1273, in which he reported that "though their beliefs are wrapped up in many lies and decorated with fictions, yet it now manifestly appears that they are near to the Christian faith and not far from the path of salvation."[29]

Besides, he reported a common conception in the hearts of all Moslems, that the faith and doctrine of Mahomet, like that of the Jews, is soon to come to an end, leaving only the faith of Christ stable and enduring as long as the world shall last.[30] Bacon had known of this belief from literary sources; and we know that there was a saying popularly attributed to Mahomet that his religion would last only as long as the dynasty of the Abbassids.[31] This dynasty had been destroyed in the sack of Baghdad in 1258, so if there was anything in the prophecy the end of Islam was at hand.

[29] William of Tripoli, *Tractatus de Statu Saracenorum,* printed in H. Prutz, Kulturgeschichte der Kreuzzüge, 1883, 573–98. The passage quoted is on p. 595.

[30] *Ibid.,* p. 596.

[31] This tradition is preserved in various forms: e.g., "The Caliphate shall abide among the children of my paternal uncle ('Abbās) and of the race of my father until they deliver it unto the Messiah"; "The government shall not cease to abide with them until they resign it into the hands of Jesus, the Son of Mary" (quoted by T. W. Arnold, *The Caliphate,* 1924, pp. 52–53).

William of Tripoli also reported criticism of the Prophet, and detected a consciousness among Moslems that they had no articulate theology.[32] He had himself, he said, baptized more than a thousand Moslems.[33] Anyone reading this report would have concluded that the field was ripe for the harvest.

While William of Tripoli reported that Islam was on the point of dissolution, there were equally hopeful signs that the Christians of the East were ready for union with their Western brethren. In 1283 a German traveler, Burchard of Mount Syon, wrote a report of his experiences. He had seen a great deal of the Latin cities which still flourished along the coast of Syria, and he had observed the varieties of Christian communities in the interior. He wrote of them with enthusiasm:

It is to be noted, and it is the simple truth, though some who speak of things they have never seen say the opposite, that the whole of the East, from the Mediterranean to India and Ethiopia, confesses and proclaims the name of Christ, except only the Saracens, and certain Turks, who live in Cappadocia. I state definitely, from what I have myself seen and heard from others who know the facts, that in every place and kingdom, except in Egypt and in Arabia, where many Saracens and other followers of Mahomet live, you will always find thirty or more Christians for one Saracen. All these overseas Christians, however, belong to oriental nations who have little skill in arms. Thus, when attacked by Saracens, Tartars, and others, they become subject to them, and buy their peace and quiet by paying tribute; and the Saracens or others who rule over them place bailiffs and tax-collectors in their lands. Hence it happens

[32] *De Statu Saracenorum*, p. 596.
[33] *Ibid.*, p. 598.

that the kingdom is called after the Saracens, though the greater part of the population are Christians, except the bailiffs and tax-collectors and their followers. I myself have seen this in Cilicia and lesser Armenia, which is subject to the lordship of the Tartars. For I was with the king of Armenia and Cilicia for three weeks. There were with him some Tartars, but all the others who belonged to the household were Christians to the number of about two hundred. I saw them flock to church, hear mass, kneel in devout prayer. Moreover, wherever they went they showed me great honor, pulling off their caps, and devoutly bowing, saluting us, and rising to us.

Many people are terrified when they hear that these countries overseas are inhabited by Nestorians, Jacobites, Maronites, Georgians, and others, who take their name from heretics whom the Church has condemned. These people believe that their followers also are heretics and follow the errors from which they take their name. But this is absolutely untrue. God forbid that it should be. They are simple men of devout behavior. I don't deny that there are some fools among them, just as the Roman Church does not lack its fools. But all the above nations, and others too many to list, have their archbishops, bishops, abbots, and other prelates, just like us, and they are called by the same names, except that among the Nestorians their chief prelate is called Iaselick, and I have learnt that his jurisdiction is of much wider extent in the East than that of the whole Western Church.[34]

Here indeed is a cheerful picture of the great world of Asia: the Christians numerous, simple-hearted men, almost Catholics; Islam weak and thinly spread, its work accomplished, awaiting in deep discouragement its expected end. As for the Mongols, for fifty years they had caused the West

[34] *Descriptio Terrae Sanctae,* printed in J. C. M. Laurent, *Peregrinationes medii aevi quatuor,* 1864, pp. 91–93.

alternating fits of terror and of hope, but now their place was becoming clear: they were at once the sustaining element in which the distant Christians had their being, and the instrument for the final destruction of Islam. We have seen the testimony of men of several different races of western Europe—Bacon an Englishman, William of Rubroek a Fleming, William of Tripoli a Syrian, Burchard of Mount Syon a German—all concurring in this general view. The short period of about thirty years, from 1260 to 1290, when this picture of the world could seem reasonably convincing to rational men, was the most hopeful period of the Middle Ages. It had its culmination in a series of Mongol embassies to the West between 1285 and 1290, which came for the express purpose of preparing for a joint attack on Islam. These embassies were led by Nestorian Christians, and in 1287 there was the unexampled spectacle of the leader of the Mongol embassy attending Mass in St. Peter's, in the presence of the Pope.[35] What a vista of endless and universal peace and unity was opened up by this picture: Islam, either destroyed or, better still, converted by philosophy; the Mongol empire stretching to the confines of China, a Christian state; and Christendom itself enriched by the philosophical tradition handed down from Greece through Moslem philosophers, to provide the one thing necessary for the fullness of Christian truth. It was a noble prospect, and one which, if only a fraction of it had come true, would radically have altered the history of the world.

[35] For this mission, see W. Budge, *The Monks of Kublai Khan*, pp. 164–97; and for the background R. Grousset, *Histoire des Croisades*, III, 707ff., and S. Runciman, *History of the Crusades*, II, 397–401.

Why it did not come true, and what the results of its failure to come true were on the intellectual outlook of Europe in the later Middle Ages, will be the subject of the next chapter.

THE MOMENT OF VISION

✳✳✳✳✳✳✳✳✳✳✳✳✳✳✳✳✳✳✳

IN THE first two chapters, I have examined the main views of Islam which were developed in western Europe up to the end of the thirteenth century. The first Biblical and unhopeful, the second imaginative and untruthful, the third philosophical and, at least for a short period, extravagantly optimistic about the near approach of world unity and the settlement of the outstanding differences between Christendom and Islam.

In this chapter I want to discuss the situation which arose when these hopes proved to be illusory. It is a long stretch to cover and a confused one, and perhaps it will simplify the structure of what I have to say if I begin by explaining that the central place in this chapter will be taken by a literary correspondence between four men of different nationalities, all writing in the ten years between about 1450 and 1460. But in order to put this debate in its correct setting, I must spend some time explaining the situation as it developed between about 1290 and the beginning of this correspondence, and finally I shall say something about the situation after 1460. Very soon after 1290 there are signs of a revulsion of feeling against the extravagant hopes of the previous thirty years. The turning point may conveniently be placed at the fall of Acre in May 1291. When the news of its fall reached Italy, Raymund Lull wrote some prophetic words which accurately summed up the hopes of the previous decades and foreshadowed the end of these hopes. "If the schismatics [the Nestorians] are brought into the fold and the Tartars converted, all the Saracens can easily be destroyed." These were the hopes that Europe had come to entertain, though we may notice that the grim Majorcan speaks now of destruction and not of conversion. But he continues, "It is much to be feared lest the Tartars receive the Law of Mahomet, for if they do this, either by their own volition or because the Saracens induce them to do so, the whole of Christendom will be in great danger." [1]

This danger was on the point of realization. The last really important and well-informed medieval traveler to Islam, writing in the last years of the thirteenth century, the Florentine Ricoldo da Montecroce, shows admirably how the tide was beginning to flow in the direction that Lull had foreseen.[2] Ricoldo was in Baghdad in 1291 when the news of the fall of Acre arrived, so he was well placed to form a judgment. The first thing that strikes us in his account of his experiences is his lack of faith in the Mongols. He saw

[1] Raymundus Lullus, *Opera Latina,* ed. schola Lullistica, 1954, fasc. iii, *Quomodo Terra Sancta recuperari potest,* p. 96.

[2] The text of Ricoldo's *Liber Peregrinationis,* on which the account which follows is based, together with a survey of his life, will be found in U. Monneret de Villard, *Il libro della Peregrinazione nelle Parti d'Oriente,* 1948.

clearly that they were beginning to turn not to Christendom, as the earlier generation had hoped and believed, but
to Islam, because, as he explains, they found it easier to
practice and easier to believe.[3] The Kurds of Turkestan had
even renounced their newly acquired Christianity in favor
of Islam, because of its greater laxity.[4] As for the Nestorians,
that large and scattered body of Eastern Christians, on
whom such high hopes had been based in the middle of the
century, he speaks of them, not as those simple men of
essentially orthodox faith we have learnt to know from the
time of the early travelers, but as men who, on the central
point of Christianity, that is to say the doctrine of the
Incarnation, were no better than Moslems.[5] And as for the
Moslems themselves, while he had a high regard for their
social virtues, and especially for their gravity of deportment,
he ignores their philosophers, and violently attacks their
doctrine as lax, confused, mendacious, irrational, violent,
obscure, and so on.[6] Nothing is said about their supposed

[3] Ricoldo notes that the Tartars, who had at first killed the Saracens
without mercy and spared the Christians, had become Moslems *cum
invenissent legem largissimam, quae quasi nullam difficultatem tenet nec
in credulitate nec in operatione.* He still found traces of the earlier inclination toward Christianity, but he had no illusions about its prospects of
success: *videtur eis quod lex Christianorum sit valde difficilis.* He also
noted that the present Khan of Persia, Argkun (1284–1291), though a
friend to the Christians, was *homo pessimus in omni scelere,* unlike his
father and grandfather (*ibid.,* p. 121).

[4] *Ibid.,* p. 123.

[5] "Positio eorum de Christo si subtiliter inspiciatur, totum misterium
Incarnationis evacuat, et de Christo fere idem sentiunt quod Sarraceni"
(p. 128).

[6] The most surprising feature of Ricoldo's eulogy of Saracen virtues is
the absence of any reference to sexual license, a stock theme of most
Western writers. On the contrary, he asserts that during all the time he

closeness to Christianity, and equally nothing about their impending end. Despite his conviction that the doctrine of Islam could be fairly easily refuted, he expresses no belief in any easy or immediate concord between the two systems of faith.

This unhopeful attitude of the learned Florentine was expressed with increasing rancor and decreasing learning by all later travelers to the Islamic countries during the next hundred years or so. The Irish Franciscan, Simon Semeonis, for example, who traveled to Palestine in 1323, was an acute observer; he had with him a copy of the Koran, and he quite often quotes it; but he cannot mention either Mahomet or the Moslems without opprobrious epithets—pigs, beasts, sons of Belial, sodomites, and so on.[7] Ten years later, an Italian, James of Verona, wrote an extensive account of his travels over much of the same ground.[8] He made many interesting observations on both the Moslem and Christian communities he met with on his travels. But the feature which must strike any reader coming to him from the thirteenth century is that his observations have no background

---

was in Persia he never heard a light song (*cantum vanitatis*) but only songs in praise of God, the law, and the Prophet (*cantum de laude Dei et de commendatione suae legis et sui prophetae*). All these virtues, however—*sollicitudo ad studium, devotio in oratione, misericordia ad pauperes, reverentia ad nomen Dei et prophetas et loca sancta, gravitas in moribus, affabilitas ad extraneos, concordia et amor ad suos*—existed in spite of the follies of their faith: *obstupuimus quomodo in lege tantae perfidiae poterant opera tantae perfectionis inveniri*. There seemed to be nothing to be done about it (pp. 131ff.).

[7] See the *Itinerarium Symeonis ab Hybernia ad Terram Sanctam*, ed. M. Esposito (*Scriptores Latini Hiberniae*, IV), 1960.

[8] *Liber Peregrinationis di Jacopo da Verone*, ed. U. Monneret de Villard, 1950.

of coherent thought. They are entirely empirical, except that
he held the view of writers of a much earlier period that
the Law of Mahomet was constructed as a colossal parody of
Christianity.[9] There was therefore no hope of any integra-
tion of the basic tenets of Islam into Christendom, and all
prospect of finding a common intellectual basis for discussion had disappeared. As James of Verona walked through
the ruins of the lately flourishing Christian cities of Acre,
Tyre, Sidon, and Tripoli, and observed that the once
populous palaces and commercial quarters were now uninhabited, except for a few wild nomads, he was filled with
gloom.[10] Military reconquest was a prospect as distant as
intellectual rapprochement. Yet, hopeless as it seemed, military measures appeared the only possible course of action.
He wrote, he said, to stir up Western Christians at least to
visit the Holy Places, if not to reconquer them and restore
them to the Faith. He called on God to hasten the moment
of reconquest.[11] But if this were to happen, it would (it
seemed) have to be God who did it, for despite the fears of
a new Crusade which he found prevalent in the East, no one
in the West seemed seriously interested.

[9] See pp. 101–6, *ibid.*, for an account of the *Lex Mahometi* with its
many curious details, all unfavorable, as the introductory sentence pre-
dicts: *Nunc dicamus de scelerata lege Mahometi, et pauca cum sit omnino
abominabilis.*

[10] The description of Acre may serve as an example: *Dolens et gemens
ipsam ingressus sum rememorans ipsam fuisse portum et utile habitaculum
Christianorum, nunc autem dirupta et dejecta et sola habitatio serpentium
et ferarum.* The towers and palaces remained, but they were uninhabited
except for a few Saracens, *pessimi et crudeles contra Christianos* (pp.
142ff.). The extent of the commercial ruin can be more vividly appreciated
in these pages than in any other account I know.

[11] *Ibid.*, p. 145.

The external reasons for a change of attitude toward Islam were strong indeed. But, as if these were not enough, they were quickly reinforced by equally important internal reasons. It is one of the frequent ironies of history that great intellectual movements so often succeed in getting official recognition and institutional backing at the very moment when they cease to have any weight in the counsels of the world. So it happened now. The schools of modern languages, for which Bacon and several other friars had been clamoring since about the year 1250 with very limited success, suddenly in 1312 were written into the official policy of the Western Church at the Council of Vienne. They were to be established in Arabic, Greek, Hebrew, and Syriac at Paris, Oxford, Bologna, Avignon, and Salamanca.[12] This

[12] The chief inspiration behind this move was Raymund Lull, the great Majorcan (c. 1235–1316) and one of the most commanding figures in the medieval study of Islam. On almost every score he deserves a much greater place in these pages than I have given him. I have refrained, partly because, with his vast output of more than 200 works, he is a special subject in himself, and partly because in all this torrential energy there seems to me a streak of madness to which I cannot do justice. He does, however, illustrate the change from the earlier period of rational systematization and hope, discussed in the last chapter, to the disillusionment of the period from 1290 onwards. Lull was a firm believer in the possibility of the rational demonstration of the Christian faith to unbelievers, and hence of the need to study the languages and habits of the countries surrounding Europe, and to maintain missions in them. In all this his attitude is similar to that of Roger Bacon. But whereas Bacon is virtually silent after 1268, Lull has expressed in poignant terms the disappointments of his later years. His efforts become increasingly frantic, his estimate of the size of the problem increasingly somber, and the official response to his appeals (with the exception of the single success at Vienne) remained frigid. He lived to see realized his fears that the Tartars would be converted to Islam, and he died in all probability a martyr. He also expressed with extreme vehemence the reaction of the late thirteenth and early fourteenth century against Averroes, whom he looked on as the personifi-

act was the last salute to a dying ideal: neither the men nor the money was at hand to give substance to the dream, and it faded away without anybody's noticing.

In many ways the years after the Council of Vienne are an ominous period in the history of Europe. For the first time in the Middle Ages we see a really distinct breach between tradition and innovation. The condemnations, following each other in rapid succession, of the views of Marsilius of Padua, of William of Ockham, of Eckhart, of the Spiritual Franciscans, of Dante's *Monarchia,* were indications of the breakdown of the unity of Western thought, which—with whatever qualifications we may care to make—was the chief feature of the previous century. In the confusion which followed this breakdown, there was no energy left to attempt to determine the place of Islam in the providential order of world history. Still less was there any desire to learn from Islam. The hospitable reception of Islamic philosophy which had marked the middle years of the thirteenth century gave way increasingly to suspicion and xenophobia. The name of Averroes became for many synonymous with infidelity, and the followers of St. Thomas saw it as his glory, not that he had learned from Averroes, but that he had humbled him.[13] This was a half-

---

cation of Islam in philosophy. For the immediate question of Lull's influence at the Council of Vienne, see B. Altaner, "Raymundus Lullus und der Sprachenkanon (can. 11) des Konzils von Vienne (1312)," *Historisches Jahrbuch,* LII, 1933, 190–219; and for an account of Lull's life and works, see *Histoire littéraire de la France,* XXIX, 1885, 1–386; M. C. Diaz y Diaz, *Index Scriptorum Latinorum medii aevi Hispanorum,* 1959, pp. 348–84.

[13] The theme of the overthrow of Averroes by St. Thomas is illustrated in several fourteenth century pictures, of which the most famous is the

truth which accurately reflected the mood of the time.

These were the marks of the new age: disbelief in the existence of allies outside Europe, deep-seated dissensions within Europe, and a comparative indifference to external enemies, especially the great enemy Islam. This last feature might seem difficult to explain, for Islam was expanding very rapidly in the early fourteenth century. But it was expanding in directions which gave Europe little immediate concern, deep into Asia and India. Once belief in the Mongols and Nestorian Christians as potential allies had been destroyed, it seemed to matter little that the Nestorians were disappearing, and that the Mongols among whom William of Rubroek had traveled were turning to Islam. The West was no longer safe, but it could afford to be indifferent.

Hence indifference and fantasy flourished once more. The Western lives of Mahomet took on a new lease of life. From having been a magician, he now became a cardinal, and his pique at not being elected to the papacy turned him into the avowed enemy of Christianity.[14] With regard to the outside world, the collecting of information gave way to the more

---

"Glorification of St. Thomas Aquinas" in St. Catherine's, Pisa, c. 1365, reproduced in R. Klibansky, *The Continuity of the Platonic Tradition during the Middle Ages*, 1939, and elsewhere. It was one of the remarkable achievements of Renan that as long ago as 1852 he saw the significance of artistic representations for the history of Averroes' reputation, and made a search for this material (*Averroès et l'Averroïsme*, pp. 238–49).

[14] This subject is discussed in an essay which I have not been able to see: E. Doutté, *Mahomet Cardinal*, 1899. See also G. Paris, *La Littérature française au moyen âge*, 3rd ed., 1905, pp. 243, 317; and *Romania*, XXXVII, 1908, 262.

congenial task of elaborating fictions, such as those which
went under the name of Sir John Mandeville and provided
fourteenth century readers with their picture of Asia and
India.[15]

Indifference is of course more difficult to detect than
fantasy. But we may see one example of it in the progress
made by the *bon mot,* or rather *mauvais mot,* first spoken
in the West by the Emperor Frederick II, that the world had
seen three great imposters, Moses, Christ, and Mahomet.[16]
Spoken in the kingdom of Sicily, the traditional home of
indifference and cynicism, this saying might cause us no
surprise. But in 1340 it was reported in Lisbon, and in the
1380s in Aragon.[17] A mere straw in the wind, but a
significant one.

At a much more respectable level, this ambiguity about
the exclusive claim of Christianity to confer the gift of

[15] See M. Letts, *Sir John Mandeville: The Man and his Book,* 1949. It
may be noted that the groundwork of fantasy and marvels had already
been well prepared by Marco Polo. The gasp of astonishment and the
mark of exclamation are never long absent from *Le Livre . . . où sont
décrites les Merveilles du Monde.*

[16] For the early history of this saying in the West, see M. Esposito,
"Una manifestazione d'incredulità religiosa nel medioevo," *Archivio
storico italiano,* ser. 7, XVI, 1931, 3–38. It can be traced back in Islam as
far as the tenth century. The evidence for the attribution of this saying
to Frederick II is very strong, but he derived it no doubt from a Moslem
source. The most interesting testimony to the state of mind expressed in
this saying is in Matthew de Acquasparta's *Quaestiones Disputatae,*
quoted by Esposito: "Erraverunt aliqui dicentes quod nulla est lex, nulla
est fides firma aut stabilis, sed in omni secta quicquid credatur, quomo-
documque vivatur, potest obtineri salus, dummodo non abhorreat a
consuetudine. . . . Istius erroris fuisse Fridericus, qui fuit imperator, qui
omnes legislatores reputabat truffatores."

[17] M. Esposito, "Les hérésies de Thomas Scotus," *Revue d'histoire
ecclésiastique,* XXXIII, 1937, 56–69.

eternal blessedness can be found at the Universities. If this ambiguity were found only in writers noted for their violence of language and eccentricity of thought, we might think no more about it. But Professor Knowles has recently drawn attention to a view maintained by a Benedictine monk, Uthred of Boldon, in the University of Oxford in the 1360s, that at the moment of death all human beings, whether Christian or Moslem, or of whatever faith, enjoyed the direct vision of God and received their everlasting judgment in the light of their response to this experience.[18] Here was a man who belonged to the most conservative of the religious orders, a doctor of divinity whose ways of thought were orthodox, laborious, and unoriginal, putting forward a view which admitted unbelievers outside Christendom to the privileges hitherto, in traditional Christian thought, exclusively reserved for Christian believers. The proposition was condemned and withdrawn, but it was significant. The growing concern about the eternal fate of unbelievers—I do not mean simply a desire to convert them, but a desire to find some means, if it were possible, of including them in the scheme of salvation—is one of the most attractive features of the period. The earlier Middle Ages had been very little, if at all, troubled by the thought that the flames of hell awaited those outside the fold. The harsh separation of the sheep from the goats was an axiom of its religious

---

[18] M. D. Knowles, "The Censured Opinions of Uthred of Boldon," *Proceedings of the British Academy,* XXXVIII, 1953. Dom Knowles, p. 315, writes: "So far as can be ascertained, this opinion was an original proposition of Uthred, and as such it entitles him to a place in the history of dogma."

life, and discountenanced all attempts to enlarge the area of Redemption. The contrary tendency appeals to every human instinct, but it also marks, for better or worse, a loosening of the cohesion of the Western world, an obscuring of its sense of separateness, and a blurring of the clear-cut line between the West and its neighbors.

John Wycliffe

The gains and losses of the fourteenth century, so far as they illustrate Western thought about Islam, may be measured by a consideration of the views of John Wycliffe. Like Roger Bacon, and for many of the same reasons, Wycliffe is a man who has been extravagantly overpraised and equally unreasonably underrated, and the latter tendency at the moment seems to be uppermost. I shall not attempt to rehabilitate him, but I think he deserves much more respect than he has recently been getting. No one can read even a little of his works without recognizing that he is a far more interesting writer than any of his academic contemporaries whose works have so far come to light. We must not allow the eccentricity and violence of some of his views to obscure the extent to which he expressed, only more fearlessly and sharply than others, the things which many people thought. His scholarship and range of knowledge, and most of his opinions, were those of his time; and for several years, until it became too dangerous to agree with him, probably a majority of that not notably revolutionary body, the University of Oxford, would have gone with him most of the way in most of what he said.

In nearly all his later writings, and especially from about 1378 to 1384, he has something to say about Islam.[19] His knowledge of Islam, like that of all his contemporaries, was slight in comparison with the knowledge of writers a hundred years earlier. He was especially weak in practical knowledge: there is no sign that he knew any of the accounts of Islam writer by the great thirteenth century travelers. Equally the Moslem philosophers were not strongly represented in his works. It was not even clear to him that Averroes was a Moslem, though he thought he had once been a follower of Mahomet.[20] Most of his knowledge came from encyclopedias—from Vincent of Beauvais, Ranulf Higden, and what he calls "another old chronicle which I lately saw." [21] But it is significant that he had read the Koran, and in this he shows his desire to become acquainted with fundamental texts.

Although he used the works of contemporaries, expressed many of their views, and suffered from many of their limitations, there was a strain of original vision in Wycliffe which forbade him to think quite as other men

---

[19] The main works in which he has something to say about Islam are the following: c. 1375, De Civili Dominio; 1378, De Ecclesia, De Veritate Sacrae Scripturae; 1379, De Officio Regis, De Potestate Papae, de Eucharistia, De Apostasia; 1381, De Blasphemia; 1382, Dialogus; 1384, Opus Evangelicum. In addition, see among his undated Polemical Works the following: De Fundatione Sectarum; Cruciata; De Christo et suo Adversario Antichristo; and among the Opera Minora: De Fide Catholica; De Vaticinatione seu Prophetia; Ad Argumenta emuli Veritatis. All these works are in the publications of the Wyclif Society, and the references which follow are to the volumes of the Society.

[20] In quoting Averroes he says of him "qui dicitur aliquando fuisse de secta Machometi" (De Veritate Sacrae Scripturae, p. 259).

[21] Ibid., pp. 250–51.

did. All the accounts of Islam we have so far studied,
whether they derived their inspiration from the Bible, or
from philosophy, or simply from the imagination, whether
they thought of the existence of Islam as a symptom of the
approaching end of the world, or as a channel for the
philosophical education of Christendom, or simply as a
falling away from the true Church, were agreed on this
one point of the utter separation between Christendom
and Islam. It was here that Wycliffe was wholly different
from his predecessors. He was different, but Uthred of
Boldon's proposition, which I have just quoted, shows
that Wycliffe was developing along a line suggested by
a much less revolutionary contemporary. Wycliffe, however, went much further. For him the main characteristics
of Islam were also the main characteristics of the Western
Church of his own day. This does not mean that he was
favorably disposed toward Islam. On the contrary. The
leading characteristics of both Islam and the Western
Church, as he saw them, were pride, cupidity, the desire
for power, the lust for possession, the gospel of violence,
and the preference of human ingenuity to the word of
God. These features in the West were the main cause
both of the divisions within Christendom and of the divi-
sion of the West from its neighbors—the division of
Avignon from Rome, of Greek from Latin, of Western
Christendom from the Nestorians and from the other
Christian communities of Asia and India, and finally of
Islam from Christianity.[22] "We Western Mahomets," he

[22] Some of the main passages in which these views are expressed are:
De Civili Dominio, iii, 74; *De Blasphemia*, 48; *De Christo et suo Adversario Antichristo* (*Polemical Works*), ii, 672.

says, referring to the Western Church as a whole, "though we are only a few among the whole body of the Church, think that the whole world will be regulated by our judgment and tremble at our command."[23] From such a view, he felt, no good could come.

These vices in the Church were, in a mysterious way, the cause of the rise of Islam, which only began with the growth of pride and avarice and the possessions of the Church.[24] And just as worldliness in the Church produced the religion of worldliness in Islam, so Islam would wither away with the reversal of this tendency within the Church, and in no other way. "I am bold to say," Wycliffe wrote on the vigil of the Annunciation, 1378, "that this antireligion will grow until the clergy returns to the poverty of Jesus Christ, and to its original state. For opposites, as Aristotle says in the fourth book of his *Meteorology,* are dissolved by their opposites, and the hill of the Lord is built by persecution and patience."[25]

Once he had got the idea of a universal Islam, a religion of worldly power, secular dominion, and self-will, opposed to the religion of suffering and poverty, both within the Church and outside it, he was able to see many ways in which this parallel was illustrated. It was the distinguishing feature of Mahomet's law that he selected from the Old and New Testaments those features which suited his purpose and rejected the rest. But then, this was pre-

[23] *Dialogus,* 91.
[24] *De Christo et suo Adversario Antichristo (Polemical Works),* ii, 672; *Ad Argumenta emuli Veritatis (Opera Minora),* 290.
[25] *De Veritate Sacrae Scripturae,* 266–67. See also *Opus Evangelicum,* i, 119.

cisely what the Possessioners within the Church had
done.[26] Again, Mahomet added his own inventions to the
Law: but the religious orders of the West had done the
same.[27] To crown all—and this was the secret of his success—Mahomet, conscious that reason was against him,
had forbidden discussion of his Law.[28] It was to be received without question. But was this not also the rule of
Canon Law with regard to papal power? And later, with
regard to the Eucharist, his enemies took refuge in ignorance with the followers of Mahomet, saying "you can
believe with safety, but you cannot safely investigate." [29]

So, at bottom, the main struggle in the world was between Evangelical Christianity on the one hand and the
spirit of Islam on the other, and the latter was found in
prelates at home as much as in Moslems abroad. From
this there followed several consequences of great importance for the placing of Islam in a universal setting. It
was a heresy, as many earlier writers had suggested; but
a heresy not only or even chiefly at a doctrinal level, but
rather at the level of morals and practice; and at this
level the Western Church was more culpable even than
Islam.[30] Moreover, since Islam was only curable by curing

[26] *De Ecclesia,* 517; *De Officio Regis,* 63; *De Fide Catholica* (*Opera
Minora*), 184.

[27] *De Blasphemia,* 84; *De Potestate Papae,* 110; *De Fundatione Sectarum*
(*Polemical Works*), i, 30.

[28] *De Veritate Sacrae Scripturae,* 261. At this date (1378) Wycliffe still
contrasted the Moslem stifling of discussion with the Christian liberty
of discussion among "prudent and grave philosophers." But later the
actual practice of the Church appeared to him no better than that of Islam.

[29] *De Eucharistia,* 118, 157, 286.

[30] *De Blasphemia,* 275; *De Apostasia,* 67, where Wycliffe asserts that

the diseases of Christendom, not only was war useless—
this was self-evident, since the impulses of war were the
very impulses which lay at the source of the disease[31]—
but even preaching and argument directed at Islam were
subordinate to the reform of the Church from within.
And finally, as a further consequence of breaking down
the rigid distinction between Christendom and Islam,
salvation was not the prerogative of Christians alone. At
this point Wycliffe repeats and develops the condemned
doctrine of Uthred of Boldon:

Just as some who are in the Church are damned, so others outside the Church are saved. If you object that, if this is so, we
cannot call the Jews unbelievers, the Saracens heretics, the
Greeks schismatics, and so on, I reply, "Man can be saved from
any sect, even from among the Saracens, if he places no obstacle
in the way of salvation. From Islam and from other sects, those
who at the moment of death believe in the Lord Jesus Christ
will be judged to be faithful Christians." [32]

We generally see Wycliffe as one of the great destructive
forces within the medieval Church, and this, as seen after
the event, is no doubt right. But Wycliffe, in his view of
Islam, summed up the results of a century in which responsible men in the West had become critical of their
society as never before, and had found it less clearly distinguished from the outside world than had previously

---

Moslems are not so *regulariter heretici* as the irreligious prelates of his
own day; *Opus Evangelicum,* i, 417–18.

[31] Wycliffe puts the wars of kingdom against kingdom in the West on
the same level as the wars of so-called Christians against Saracens (*Opus
Evangelicum,* i, 114).

[32] *De Fide Catholica* (*Opera Minora*), 112.

been hoped and believed. Wycliffe's major conclusions about Islam did not have much, or perhaps any, general influence, because the system of thought in which they cohered was rigorously repressed. But the moral and intellectual atmosphere which made his conclusions seem plausible continued, either by repulsion or attraction, to affect the whole future of medieval thought about Islam. To take only one quite trifling example. That gossipy old man, Thomas Gascoigne, an Oxford character of the middle of the fifteenth century who certainly loathed Wycliffe and all his works, is found writing in his commonplace book: "I have heard a certain man, who is worthy of credence, say that he heard among the pagans and Saracens that there were three causes for their not wishing to be converted to the faith of Jesus Christ: firstly, the diversity and contradiction of opinion among Christians in various sects and on various subjects; secondly, the evil lives of the Christians; and thirdly, the ill-faith of the Christians, and especially of the Venetians and Genoese." [33]

This explanation, which points inwards at Christians themselves and their own deficiencies as the explanation for their lack of success, and for the persistent deviation of Islam from the truth, is the mark of the new age.

II

One thing, however, which became clear in the fifteenth

---

[33] Thomas Gascoigne, *Loci e Libro Veritatum,* ed. J. E. Thorold Rogers, 1881, p. 102–3. This extract probably dates from a period shortly after 1450.

century was that something would have to be done about
Islam. When Wycliffe was writing, it was still possible,
but only just possible, to treat Islam as a moral but not
a physical danger. He could write as he did, as if there
was little to choose between prelates and Moslems, because
neither prelates nor Moslems, whatever their vices, were
threatening the country with the sword. The growth of
Islam was a fact, but it was a distant prospect. Now it
grew ominously nearer. Five years after Wycliffe's death
the Serbs collapsed before the Turkish attack; by the end
of the fourteenth century the Turks were masters of the
Balkans, except for Bosnia and Albania. Then, as often
happens, the danger failed to develop. There was time to
indulge in false hopes. But, in the end, under massive
blows Constantinople fell; the Turks stood on the Adriatic;
Hungary was threatened with destruction. By 1460, the
outposts of western Europe, of Latin Christendom, had
been reached and breached.

The reaction to these long-expected events was a mixture
of fear and hope. There was little reason for the latter,
but the fall of Constantinople had at least solved the
obstinate Greek problem that had so long eluded the
efforts of statesmen. There was a hope—illusory, as the
event showed—that the elimination of this domestic enemy
might have beneficial results, and that the direct con-
frontation of the West with Islam might also revive the
ancient Crusading spirit. These were the possibilities before statesmen in the mid-fifteenth century. They prepared
for a Crusade, and hoped that a Crusade would not be
necessary, perhaps because at bottom they knew it would

not be possible. This was the situation which confronted
the four statesmen with whom we shall now be concerned.

They were men of about the same age, all bishops, three
of them cardinals or about to become cardinals; one was
a Franciscan, one was to become pope.[34] By the middle
of the fifteenth century they had all had their full share
of troubles. The most obvious difference between them
was their nationality: John of Segovia was a Spaniard,
Nicholas of Cusa a German, Jean Germain a Frenchman,
and Aeneas Silvius an Italian. But they had one thing in
common: they had all been through the chastening experience of the Council of Basel. The Council had forced
men—able, academic men, not prone to decisive action—
to take sides, and one way or another they had all suffered in the process. Two of them had suffered in going
through the unpleasant experience of changing sides; the
third in the even more unpleasant experience of not
changing sides; only the Frenchman had been untroubled
by doubts. This experience was extraordinarily formative
in their lives. They had all (except the Frenchman) been
strong supporters of Conciliar views, and even those who
abandoned them did not abandon their sympathy with

[34] John of Segovia was born about 1400; created a cardinal by the
anti-pope Felix V in 1440; titular archbishop of Caesarea in 1453; retired
to the priory of Aiton in Savoy in 1453; died in May 1458. Nicholas of
Cusa was born in 1401; created a cardinal by Nicholas V in 1448; died
in 1464. Jean Germain was born about 1400; bishop of Nevers and first
chancellor of the Order of the Golden Fleece in 1430; bishop of Châlon-
sur-Saône, 1436; died in 1461. Aeneas Silvius was born in 1405; Secretary
to the Council of Basel, 1436–1440, and to the anti-pope Felix V, 1440–
1442; Bishop of Trieste, 1447, and of Siena, 1450; Cardinal, 1456; Pope,
1458; died, 1464.

the other side. They had learnt a habit of conciliation; and conciliation had already achieved more inside Europe than could have been achieved by any other method. It had prepared the way for the re-establishment of Papal unity, it had brought the Hussite movement to an end, it had briefly brought about the union of the Greek and Latin churches. These were the results of interminable wearisome negotiations. Only the problem of Islam remained as a major physical and intellectual challenge to Europe's peace of mind and body. In what ways could the experience of the last few decades be applied to the solution of this age-old problem? This was the question foremost in the minds of all four statesmen in the decade from 1450 to 1460, and their answers are what we must now examine.

John of Segovia

We shall begin with John of Segovia. He had started as a professor at Salamanca, and from there he went to the Council of Basel in 1433.[35] He was a strong supporter of the authority of the Council and wrote its history—a vast work which occupies 2500 folio pages in the printed edition.[36] In the end he found himself on the wrong side as an adherent of the anti-Pope, and his last years were spent in retirement at a small monastery in Savoy, a

[35] The main incidents of his life, especially so far as our subject is concerned, are sketched in D. Cabanelas Rodriguez, *Juan de Segovia y ed problema islamica*, 1952. For his relations with Nicholas of Cusa, and the latter's reply to his proposals for meeting the Islamic danger, see R. Klibansky and H. Bascour, *Nicolai de Cusa De Pace Fidei* (*Mediaeval and Renaissance Studies*, III, Supplement), 1956.

[36] *Historia gestorum generalis synodi Basiliensis,* in *Monumenta Conciliorum generalium saec. XV,* vols. II–IV.

useless and, in a worldly sense, a defeated man. Here he devoted himself to the study of the Islamic question, and during the last five years before his death in 1458 he did two things: he made a new translation of the Koran, and he tried to interest his distinguished friends in his plans for solving the whole problem. Both these projects require a brief consideration, and first of all the translation of the Koran, which was the foundation of his larger plans.[37]

There are three questions to be asked here: Why did he think a new translation was necessary? What difficulties did he come up against, and why are these significant? How did he propose to use his work when it was finished?

On the first question, it must be recognized that all translations are more or less unsatisfactory, but the special criticism that John of Segovia made of the old translation of the Koran of Peter the Venerable was that it introduced into the text the ideas of the Latins, and used words and notions proper to the Christian world but not to that of Islam. John of Segovia may not have been quite realistic in thinking that a translation could be made without this kind of contamination. He seems to have thought that by keeping to the order of words and sections, and by forming his style on that of the Koran, he could avoid the weaknesses of which he was conscious in the older work. In this he was perhaps wrong; but there are degrees of contamination, and he was at least seriously concerned, as previously controversialists had seldom been, not to

[37] The translation is lost, but the Prologue to it setting out John of Segovia's aims and difficulties is preserved, and printed by D. Cabanelas, *Juan de Segovia*, pp. 279–302.

misrepresent, however slightly, the thought of the rival religion. We shall soon see why this was so important to him.

But before looking further, we may take a brief look at his difficulties. Even if his intentions did not command respect, the difficulties which he faced and overcame would do so. Nothing brings more clearly before our eyes the decline in the serious interest in Islam during the previous century and a half than the great difficulty he had in finding anyone in Europe in 1453 who knew Arabic. The Spanish Moslems were now in the same position as the Spanish Christians six hundred years earlier: they had largely abandoned their language and culture for that of their conquerors. It took John of Segovia two years to secure both an Arabic text of the Koran and a Moslem jurist from Salamanca who was willing to come to Savoy to help in the translation. They toiled together for several months, and then the Moslem insisted on going back to Spain to his newly married wife. The main work was finished, but John of Segovia still hoped to make improvements. He asked the Minister-General of his own Order, the Franciscans, to find an Arabic scholar. He himself looked far and wide. But he never succeeded in getting a replacement; and so far as we know, the work never received its final revision. Despite all the projects of the thirteenth century, and the decree of the Council of Vienne in 1312, there was not a single Christian Arabic scholar to be found in Europe.

What purpose was to be served by all this elaborate labor? John of Segovia's purpose differed in some important ways from that of earlier controversialists. In the first place he wanted to bring the discussion down to fundamental issues. He thought that earlier writers had been bothered by too many inessential problems—the morals of Mahomet, the logical refutation of his claim to be a prophet, and so on. But the only really important question was this: Is the Koran the word of God or not? If, by a simple examination of the text, it can be shown to contain contradictions, confusions, errors, traces of composite authorship, these should—so he thought—convince anyone that it was not what it claimed to be. Now of course this could not be done if texts were quoted which turned out to be mistranslations, or which themselves introduced the confusions alleged to be found in the Koran. A completely accurate text was therefore the very first requirement.

In this program of textual accuracy and criticism we can recognize a symptom of the Renaissance, in contrast to Roger Bacon's program of philosophical discussion. The brisk syllogisms of Bacon were to be replaced by facts; critical scholarship was to take the place of logical gymnastics. But all this work would be quite useless unless it could be brought to the notice of those for whom it was intended. John of Segovia had a new idea also about how this should be done, and he wrote to his influential friends to enlist their support. We must now examine the plan which he outlined and the response he elicited.

Much the longest of these letters to his friends is the one he wrote to Nicholas of Cusa, the friend of earlier days. To him he poured forth his ideas in a copious stream—so copious that no one has yet found the courage to print them.[38] He started with the same basic thesis as that of Bacon, a fellow Franciscan; and in many ways we may look on him as Bacon's successor. This thesis was that war could never solve the issue between Christendom and Islam. Bacon had pointed to the evil effects of war on the conquered, and to the unlikelihood of success. John of Segovia had a different reason, which shows a certain affinity to that of Wycliffe. War was the natural mode of expression of Islam, which was founded on a doctrine of conquest. But this was contrary to the essence of Christianity; therefore Christendom must always be at a disadvantage in this kind of struggle. It was therefore only by peaceful means that Christendom could win, because only then was it true to itself.

But what were these peaceful means? Bacon, in common with all his Franciscan contemporaries, seems to have thought that when once the arguments against Islam had been formulated they would require no real discussion: they were self-evident, and it could be left to missionaries and preachers to spread their influence. John of Segovia saw that this was mistaken. Preaching would never be allowed except in territory already reconquered from

[38] I am indebted to Dom Bascour, Dr. Klibansky, and Mlle. M. T. d'Alverny for their kindness in procuring for me microfilms of the four existing manuscripts of John of Segovia's letter: Salamanca University MSS. 19, pars ix, foll. 1–17, and 55, foll. 126–56; Vatican MS. Lat. 2923, foll. 4–35; Paris, Bibl. Nat. MS. Lat. 3650, foll. 1–37. The list of contents and conclusion of the letter are printed by D. Cabanelas, pp. 303–10.

Islam, and since he had excluded war he had excluded the possibility of reconquest on a large scale. He was, I think, the first man of peace to grasp that missions to convert Islam were doomed to failure. The first problem to be faced was therefore the problem of a new kind of communication. The main purpose of his letters was to suggest a new approach. To describe this he used an old word in a new form, and with a new sense. It is a word which has come in our own day to be heavy with meaning— the word "conference" or, as John of Segovia accurately, if pedantically, put it, *contraferentia*.[39]

With regard to this new method of persuasion, he made one far-sighted observation: the conference (he said) would have served a useful purpose even if it did not achieve the end for which it was proposed—that is to say, the conversion of the Moslems. In his rather long-winded way, he listed thirty advantages which might be expected even if it failed in its main object. Now this again was quite a new conception. The traditional view was that discussion with the infidel could only be justified by conversion. But John of Segovia saw many partial and practical advantages, apart from this desirable end: he saw the conference as an instrument with a political as well as a strictly religious function, and in words which will

[39] This word *contraferentia* does not appear to be found in any other author, nor do there appear to be any medieval examples of the word *conferentia* being used in the modern sense. The nearest approach to the modern meaning, quoted by Du Cange from a letter of the Master of the Hospital about the siege of Rhodes by the Turks, seems to be *conferentia armorum* or "skirmish."

strike a chord in modern breasts he exclaimed that even
if it were to last ten years it would be less expensive and
less damaging than war.

Nicholas of Cusa

John of Segovia judged his man well in writing at such
length to Nicholas of Cusa. He could not have found a
more sympathetic listener. Nicholas was in philosophy a
Platonist, in temperament pacific and moderate, in purpose deeply committed to the search for unity. In earlier
years he had been one of the chief negotiators with the
Hussites and the Greeks, and for many years he had been
collecting all he could find on the Islamic controversy.[40]
He had recently written a work, his *De Pace Fidei,* a
dialogue between representatives of the leading religions
of the world, in which he tried to embrace what was good
in the religions of all peoples and to see through the details
to the inner core of truth and unity. Moreover—and this
for the present purpose was of special importance—he
was a textual critic of outstanding power. He was one of
the earliest men of his time to treat historical documents
in a way that would win the approval of a modern scholar.
He already had several notable successes to his credit in
this field—much the most important being the demonstration that the *Donation of Constantine* was a forgery
of a later age.[41] His cautious spirit renounced the victory

[40] For Nicholas' account of his interest in the subject since about 1435,
see his *Cribratio Alchoran,* in the edition of his works, Basel, 1565, pp.
879–80.

[41] This admirable example of historical argument is in his *De Con-
cordantia Catholica,* iii, 2, ed. G. Keller, 1959, pp. 328–37, where further
references will be found.

of declaring the demonstration complete, but it convinced his contemporaries, and it puts most of the arguments that still convince us today. So as a philosopher, as a man, as a negotiator, and as a historian, Nicholas of Cusa was very much the man whom John of Segovia was looking for. He took up John of Segovia's plans in a vigorous and practical fashion. For instance, he suggested preparations for the Conference. He wanted to have merchants summoned from Cairo, Alexandria, Armenia, and Greece, who would describe at first hand the ideas and practices of Islam. And when materials had been collected, he wanted to have intermediaries sent from the West to Islamic countries, preferably, he says, temporal princes, whom the Turks prefer to priests.[42] In this way the preparations for the great conference could take place.

Above all this, in the years after he had received John of Segovia's plan, he read the main works of the earlier controversy; and finally, in 1460, he wrote one of his most typical productions: the *Cribratio Alchoran*. In this *Sieving of the Koran,* he carried out in detail that plan of systematic literary, historical, and philological examination which John of Segovia had desired.

He treated the Koran essentially as he had treated the *Donation of Constantine,* but at much greater length.[43] He tried to break it up into its various elements, and he discovered, or thought he had discovered, that there were three strands in the Koran. The first, a basic Nestorian Christianity; second, anti-Christian sentiments introduced

---

[42] *Epistula ad Joannem de Segovia,* in Klibansky and Bascour (above, n. 35), p. 97.

[43] In the Basel edition of 1565 it occupies pp. 879–932.

by the Jewish adviser of Mahomet; and third, corruptions introduced by Jewish "correctors" after Mahomet's death. I do not suppose that this analysis of the text of the Koran has any value now, though it correctly identifies some of the main intellectual influences in it. But Nicholas of Cusa's method for limiting the area of dispute and defining the issues is important. Like John of Segovia, he abandoned the philosophical ground, and he tried to carry further the plan of discovering in the Koran itself the issues which separated Islam and Christendom, treating it as a document written in good faith, with a character and virtues of its own. In this way he hoped that he had defined and limited the area of dispute. He reduced it essentially to a dispute between Western Christianity and Nestorian Christianity, a heresy which erred in the relatively minor matter of the mode of the union of God with the human nature of Christ. The work is immensely laborious to read, and unlike Nicholas' discussion of the *Donation of Constantine* it will not convince a modern reader. But it was a first attempt to provide a scientific basis for that fundamental criticism of the text which was to be the first step toward the great conference envisaged by John of Segovia.

Jean Germain

Not all of John of Segovia's friends accorded his plan the same friendly reception that Nicholas of Cusa did. But they differed about it in different ways.

The least sympathetic of his correspondents was Jean Germain, bishop of Châlon, Chancellor of the Order of the Golden Fleece.[44] In addressing his project in this direction John of Segovia showed his determination to persist, however unlikely success might be. Jean Germain had devoted his life to a purpose precisely the opposite of that of the Salamancan doctor. He too deplored the indifference of Christendom to the Islamic peril. But his remedy was not to investigate afresh the way of peace. He preached a return to more warlike and spirited virtues, as depicted in the epics of the early Crusades. He had recently addressed the king of France in this vein:

Let us revive the spirit of Godfrey of Bouillon, of Philip the Conqueror King of France, of St. Louis. If you do this, the whole world will shout "Honor, glory, and victory to Charles King of France, the Victorious, the new David, the new Constantine, the new Charlemagne, who after all the conquests granted him by God has used them for the relief of the Holy Catholic Faith, and to his own honor and glory and everlasting good name." Amen.[45]

His plan was to revive the primitive virtues of these epic heroes, to stop the rot in Christendom through chivalry and discipline and by the suppression of heresy and error. It was not a bad plan, if only there was the faintest chance of its being carried out. The worst that can be said of Jean Germain is that he demanded virtues more easily expressed in ceremonial and symbolism than in deeds, and more flattering to the inclinations of a

[44] For Jean Germain, see G. Doutrepont, *La Littérature française à la cour des Ducs de Bourgogne,* 1909, where his works are discussed; also, Ch. Schefer, "Le discours du voyage d'oultremer au tres victorieux roi Charles VII prononce en 1452 par Jean Germain, eveque de Châlon," *Revue de l'Orient latin,* III, 1895, pp. 303–42.

[45] *Ibid.,* 342.

wealthy court than to the world at large. The one practical object to which he was deeply committed was the
Crusade, and most of his considerable energies were devoted to preparing the minds of rulers and people for
this longed-for event.

He can scarcely therefore have been pleased when he
received a few days before Christmas 1455 an enormous
budget of letters and treatises from John of Segovia, intended to inculcate the futility of war and the necessity
for finding a peaceful solution to the problem of Islam.[46]
He replied on 26 December that the Christmas festivities
had prevented his reading the whole packet. Still in the
glow of the holiday season, he encouraged John of
Segovia's researches, but he felt bound to point out that
the Turk was continuing his advance and that the whole
world would be in suspense until he was resisted. In another letter he developed this argument in a more bellicose
spirit.[47] The Holy War, he asserted, had long been con-
secrated by the decisions of popes and the practice of kings;
the Roman Church had given its authority and its indul-
gences to those who took part in it; it was supported by
the Old Testament, and by a long line of Christian heroes;
a new Crusade was in course of preparation; nothing
must be done to weaken the military purpose of western
Europe. As against this practical policy, what did John

[46] John of Segovia's letter, dated 18 December 1455, is printed in D.
Cabanelas (above, n. 35), pp. 325–28; the reply of 26 December is on
pp. 329–30.

[47] This letter does not appear to be preserved, but there is a mammoth
reply to it by John of Segovia in Vatican MS. Lat. 2923, foll. 40–136,
analyzed by D. Cabanelas, pp. 197–223.

of Segovia offer? A way of peace. But before this could be tried, the consent of the Moslem princes must be obtained. And how was this to be done? The Prophet of Islam had forbidden all discussion of doctrine, and the history of earlier attempts at discussion had shown that they were bound to fail. A course of action so repugnant to Christian sentiment would only be justified by a sure hope of success. But, whereas the fruits would be small or nonexistent, the damage to be expected was certain.

So Jean Germain wrote, as a straightforward prelate chiefly concerned with the correct ordering of Christendom and not with the subtleties of debate. It must be recognized that much of what he says is unanswerable. And we may also recognize that under the surface of the argument there were two points where he and John of Segovia were in fundamental disagreement. First of all, Jean Germain was only interested in Christendom and in attempting to rally it to a sense of its own identity: above all, he hated those Christians—merchants and others, in increasing numbers—who traveled in Islam and came back with scruples and criticisms of the Christian faith.[48] Unlike John of Segovia, he feared the contamination of discussion. And unlike John of Segovia, he placed no confidence in that consensus of reasonable and well-informed men which had been the basis of Conciliar thought. He looked rather to the prince, fortified by the teaching of bishops like himself.[49] Long

---

[48] Jean Germain had made this point in the Preface to his *Dialogue of a Christian and a Saracen,* written in 1450 (Schefer, p. 303, and Doutrepont, p. 247).

[49] See especially his *Deux pans de la Tapisserie Chrétienne,* 1457, portraying "la conduyte et maniere comme les loyaulx chrestiens militans,

ago, when he first became Chancellor of the Order of the Golden Fleece, he had changed, or tried to change, the hero of the Order from Jason, the pagan hero of legend, to Gideon, the Jewish leader in the wars with the Philistines. He saw in the Fleece not that Golden Fleece of romance but the fleece of Gideon which symbolized the Christian mystery. If Europe could once again have warlike and religious rulers, all would yet be well.

Aeneas Silvius

There is one last correspondent of John of Segovia who also placed his reliance on the ruler, though he expressed this reliance in quite a different way. In the last month of his life John of Segovia took up his pen to address the rising star of the Papal curia, an Italian this time, and the most famous humanist of his day, Aeneas Silvius.[50] This letter was John of Segovia's final effort. He was ill; he could scarcely hold his pen; he was near to death. But it was important that this effort should be made. John of Segovia exerted himself to please his correspondent. He praised the speeches in those now distant German Diets in which Aeneas had attempted to inspire Europe to resist the Moslem. But he reminded him of the Evangelical warning against meeting twenty thousand men with only ten thousand. Let him not forget that there are generally more Saracens than Christians. And at a deeper level, let him

---

pelerins et chevalereux conquerans doivent tendre à triumpher." For a description of this work, see Doutrepont, p. 252.

[50] For John of Segovia's letter to Aeneas Silvius, see D. Cabanelas, pp. 343–49. Vatican MS. Lat. 2923 is probably the manuscript of treatises which accompanied this letter (*ibid.*, p. 232n).

remember that the gift of Christ to the Church was peace, not war.

This is the general content of the letter, and we can imagine that it made some impression on Aeneas. Some of the points no doubt appealed to him as a humanist, interested in literary criticism. But the letter made no appeal to him at all as a man of action and a statesman. He could not reply to the dying John of Segovia. But his effective reply to his ideas was a letter sent in 1460 to the conqueror of Constantinople, Mahomet II.[51] This letter is a magnificent composition. In its splendor of language, in its worldly wisdom, in the skill with which the arguments are directed to the ruling passion of the Ottoman for power, in its concentration on essentials, and in the effective marshaling of the rational defenses of Christianity, it is a masterpiece. There was nothing in it to offend the susceptibilities of a barbarian or a gentleman. The whole work is compounded of clarity, vigor, and good sense, expressed with great urbanity of manner, and incisiveness of argument. The one thing which it lacks is any depth of sincerity. He wrote rather as a lawyer with a brief than as a man speaking from the heart. But from the point of view of a European statesman it is hard to say that the attempt at persuasion in this letter was not worth making.

The letter begins with a magnificent account of the strength of the kingdoms of Western Christendom, which has no parallel that I can think of before Gibbon's great

[51] Besides the old editions, there is a new edition of the letter by G. Toffanin, *Pio II: Lettera a Maometto II*, 1953. The references which follow are made to this edition.

eulogy of the West in his *Decline and Fall of the Roman Empire*. I have already cited this passage, which embodies superbly the pride of Europe at the height of its supremacy in the world. The situation was far different in 1460 with the Turk roaring into Europe. Yet in the face of all disaster Pius II managed to express the pride and confidence of superior civilization. "You are not" he says, "so ignorant of our affairs that you do not know the power of the Christian people—of Spain so steadfast, Gaul so warlike, Germany so populous, Britain so strong, Poland so daring, Hungary so active, and Italy so rich, high-spirited, and experienced in the art of war." [52] Let the Turk not suppose, from the easy successes of the last few years, that he can hope to overcome the nations of Europe. He has not yet begun his real task. Then Pius goes on:

It is a small thing, however, that can make you the greatest and most powerful and most famous man of your time. You ask what it is. It is not difficult to find. Nor have you far to seek. It is to be found all over the world—a little water with which you may be baptized, and turn to the Christian sacraments and believe the gospel. Do this, and there is no prince in the world who will exceed you in glory, or equal you in power. We will call you emperor of the Greeks and of the East. The land which you now occupy by force you will then hold by right, and all Christians will reverence you and make you their judge. It is impossible for you to succeed while you follow the Moslem law. But only turn to Christianity and you will be the greatest man of of your time by universal consent.[53]

"Perhaps," the argument continues, "you do not wish to give up your religion and become a Christian. But con-

[52] Toffanin, p. 110.
[53] *Ibid.*, pp. 113–14.

sider. There are many points of agreement between Christians and Moslems: one God, the creator of the world; a
belief in the necessity for faith; a future life of rewards and
punishments; the immortality of soul; the common use of
the Old and New Testaments; all this is common ground.
We only differ about the nature of God." [54] And here he
gives an explanation in rational and unemotional terms of
the points of difference between the two faiths. Having
done this with noble felicity of phrase, he goes on to some
of the charges made against the Christians. In the first place
there is the charge of corrupting the Bible. On the basis
of textual history he easily shows how unlikely a charge
this is, and he follows up his explanation by setting
Mahomet II a small problem in textual criticism to emphasize its unlikelihood. Are the old texts of the Old
Testament likely to be more corrupt than those newer texts
known to Mahomet and his followers? And if the texts
of the Greeks, Jews, and Gentiles agree against those of the
Saracens, which is likely to be right? [55] By scholarly standards his arguments here are irreproachable.

[54] I summarize the argument of pp. 125–29. The transition from
political to religious arguments is made with very great skill, using the
example of ancient rulers and philosophers to bridge the formidable gap
between the splendor of the world and the poverty of the Gospels. No
summary can do justice to this forensic skill.

[55] "Quaerimus ex te, magne princeps, si te iudice duo rationum codices
afferantur, quorum alter ex altero transcriptus existat, et in eo de quo est
facta transcriptio 'Sempronius mille debere talenta' scriptus est; in
exemplari 'duo millia'. Cui potius fidem dabis? Aut non exemplo potius
quam examplari? . . . Rursus ex te quaerimus: quatuor inveniuntur
rationum libri apud quatuor negotiatores, Seium, Gaium, Titium et
Sempronium. In quo quem Sempronius producit 'creditor ipse Lucii in
centum talentis' scriptus invenitur; in aliis 'debitor'. Cui credes? Quid
respondebis? An non tres libros uni praeferres?" (pp. 158–59).

Then finally: "if there were nothing else against your law, this alone would be sufficient to condemn it, that your legislator forbade it to be discussed." He was, he allows, a wise and ingenious man; he knew that his position could not be defended by reason, and he rightly calculated the assets which he had. But it is only by a misuse of language that we can give to his system the proud name of Law. "Does this shock you? Then hear the true nature of Law. Law is reason in action. What is against reason is against law. But your legislator forbids reasoning, therefore what he says cannot be reasonable, neither can it be a law." [56] Thus, in concluding his argument with an appeal to reason, Pius II turned against Islam that feature in its law which Wycliffe also had selected as the crucial point of identity between the Prophet of Islam and the Mahomets of the Western Church. But he expressed the self-confidence of the West in the superiority of its classical and Christian heritage, in contrast to Wycliffe, who had made articulate the disillusion that lay beneath the surface. In the circumstances of the time, the confidence must have appeared foolhardy; in the light of later events it was half-prophetic.

I cannot withhold my admiration from this production. It is the work of a statesman, a humanist, and a man of the world, going back to earlier and more primitive arguments than any we have so far encountered, to the kind of arguments of political prudence which convinced Constantine and Clovis. But in his arrogant and intellectual way, instead of the promise of miraculous intervention which accompanied the political prudence of Constantine and Clovis,

[56] *Ibid.*, pp. 165–66.

Aeneas Silvius made his appeal only to reason and practical good sense, set off in all the splendor of Renaissance rhetoric. Yet it was, of course, unsuccessful, and perhaps it deserved to be so.

III

We are coming to the end of our course, and there is little now to do but to draw together the threads in the controversy we have just examined, and to take a final look forward and backward. I have called the period of about ten years, from about 1450 to 1460, when our four scholars and statesmen were at work on the problem of Islam, the moment of vision. The vision was contradictory and evidently in many ways deceptive, but I think it can be claimed that it was larger, clearer, and more lifelike than at any previous moment, or any later one for several centuries at least. The writers of this period, by a great effort, had made themselves masters of the knowledge of the thirteenth century; and to this they added the wider experience and capacity for self-criticism of the fourteenth. They saw the full complexity of the problem, and they saw it as an urgent reality that required an answer. They eschewed grandiose attempts to give Islam a distinct role in world history. But, at the other end of the scale, they were all determined to cut through trivialities and unnecessary detail, and get to the central issues. They differed widely about the goal to be reached and the way to reach it, but they tried to be simple, comprehensive, and effective. In the mere fact that they differed they show an advance on their predecessors; and despite their differences they agree in this: they appealed to practical reason and common sense rather than to refined and unsubstantial speculations.

They got to grips with each other, but they failed to get to grips with Islam. Neither the conference desired by John of Segovia and Nicholas of Cusa, nor the Crusade desired by Jean Germain and Aeneas Silvius, still less the latter's appeal to the Sultan Mahomet II, had any future. The advance of Islam on the Eastern frontier continued and was not halted till the middle of the sixteenth century; Islamic power continued to grow in the Mediterranean, and the danger that Moslems in Syria would join hands with Moors in Spain persisted for many years. Crusade and argument, preaching and persuasion, alike faded into the background. As the Turkish danger reached its height and Islam threatened to engulf Europe, there was one last outburst of the medieval apocalyptic prophesying, similar to that of Eulogius and Paul Alvarus in ninth century Spain and Joachim of Fiore in Italy in the late twelfth century. In 1542 the Turks had overrun Hungary, the first great kingdom of western Europe to be destroyed by external attack since the barbarian invasions over a thousand years earlier. This was the first reversal of the expansive movement which had added new kingdoms on the eastern frontier of Europe in the tenth century. The reaction of the King of France had been to ally himself with the Turk. At any moment it seemed that Germany also might succumb.

Luther

It was at this point that the aging Luther, now an angry old man, made as a tract for the times a translation in his

own vigorous German of one of the great anti-Islamic works
of the thirteenth century, Ricoldo da Montecroce's *Con-
futatio Alchoran*.[57] To this translation he added a preface
and appendix in which—probably without knowing it—he
gave powerful expression to one well-established medieval
tradition of thought, that of despair about the possibility of
any political or intellectual solution for the problem of
Islam. Luther was persuaded that the Moslems could not be
converted: their hearts were hardened, they despised the
Scriptures, they rejected argument, they clung to the tissue
of lies of the Koran.[58] This was only what Jean Germain
had said in advocating the renewal of the Crusade. But, in
Luther's view, war was useless against Islam so long as the
West remained in its sins: "God will never give us victory
when such people as those we have fight for us." In rejecting
war as a solution he was with Roger Bacon, Wycliffe, John
of Segovia, and probably the majority of men of intellect
since the thirteenth century. But unlike them, and unlike
anyone in the West since the ninth century, he looked

---

[57] *Verlegung des Alcoran, Bruder Richardi Prediger Ordens, ver-
deudscht, durch D. Mar. Lu.,* Wittemberg, 1542. Luther's Preface contains
several curious illustrations of the low state of Islamic studies and the
short-lived effect of the work of the previous century. He says that he had
long ago read Ricoldo's book but that he did not credit its assertions that
men could believe such follies. He thought it simply another example of
the fantasies of papal superstition. He wanted to read the Koran but he
could find no Latin translation. Then, on Shrove Tuesday 1542, a translation came into his hands and he saw at once that Ricoldo had been
speaking the truth. Thereupon he translated Ricoldo's work into German.
[58] "Denn es bezeuget auch dieser Richard, das die Mahometischen nicht
zu bekeren sint, aus der Ursache, sie sind so hart verstockt, das sie fast
alle unsers Glaubens Artickel spotten und hönisch verlachen, als werens
Nerrische, von unmüglichen dingen gewesche" (fol. B).

forward to the probability that Christendom would be engulfed in Islam. He wrote to strengthen the faith of those Christians who might find themselves in this condition. The success of Turks and Saracens over so many hundreds of years did not show that they enjoyed the favor of God: they were only fulfilling the prophecy that the blood of Christ must be shed from the beginning of the world to the end. So (he says) we must let the Turks and Saracens work their will, as men on whom the wrath of God has come, provided we stay in God's grace and observe His word and sacraments.[59]

Luther wrote as if he were a man in the twilight of Christendom before the long night, and, as he looked into the future, he asked whether Mahomet and his followers were the final Antichrist. Like Joachim of Fiore, he answered No. Islam was too gross and irrational for this mighty role: the true and final, subtle and insidious Antichrist must come from within the Church; he was none other than the Pope himself.[60] This had been the picture also of Joachim and of much late medieval apocalyptic, though Luther added thereto his own theological hostility. For him and them, Christendom was caught in the grip of an external and an even more formidable internal enemy.

[59] "Also müssen wir die Turcken Sarracenen mit irem Mahomet lassen faren, als uber die der zorn Gottes, bis ans ende komen ist (wie S. Paulus von den Iüden sagt). Und dencken wie wir erhalten werden und bey Gottes gnaden bleiben mügen, damit wir nicht mit dem Mahmet verdampt werden" (fol. Aiiii^v).

[60] "Und ich halt der Mahmet nicht fur den Endechrist. Er machts zu grob . . . Aber der Bapst bey uns ist der rechte Endechrist, der hat den hohen, subtilem, schönen gleissenden Teuffel. Der sitzt inwendig in der Christenheit" (fol. X).

To succeed against the external enemy, it must first re-
nounce the internal enemy.[61] Till this time there could be
no counsel but to suffer. So Wycliffe too had said.[62]

Here then we reach intellectually the final dissolution of
the idea of Christendom as an organic unity overcoming
its external enemies by argument or force. What actually
happened of course was neither the dissolution foreseen by
Luther nor the triumph which so many others had planned
and striven for. So far as Islam was concerned, their plans
came to nothing, but the habits of mind acquired in the
long struggle for comprehension had an outlet elsewhere,
and nowhere more fruitfully than in the Salamancan doc-
tors, of whom John of Segovia had been one of the earliest
luminaries. They turned their thoughts from Islam to the
Indies, and attempted in the same spirit of rational moderation to discover the principles to be followed in solving the
problems of the new age as westward the course of empire
took its way. So far as the Islamic problem was ever solved,
it was solved by events and not by thoughts or projects,
however noble. The practical result of so much intellectual
effort was meager in the extreme. But as a chapter in the

[61] "Sollen wir nu gluck haben wider den Mahmet, den eusserlichen
Feind der Christenheit, so werden wir zuvor müssen dem inwendigen
Feinde, den Endechrist, mit seinem Teuffel absagen, durch rechtschaffene
Busse . . ." (fol. Xiii).

[62] Like Wycliffe, Luther also saw the Islamization of the West in the
typical products of the Middle Ages: "Und zwar ists nicht viel besser bey
uns Christen auch gangen. Denn da sind so viel Lugen in unsern
Alcoranen, Descretalen, Lugenden, Summen und unzelichen Buchern, da
doch niemand weis woher sie komen, wenn sie angefangen, wer die
Meister seien" (fol. V). Likewise in the refusal to investigate on the plea
that "non potest omnium ratio reddi" (fol. V^v) the medieval church had
shown its affinity to Islam.

history of European experience it has a notable place. It has taken us from the Biblical exegesis of Bede and the Carolingian scholars to the irrepressible imaginative creations of the early twelfth century. We have risen to the bold and hopeful speculations of the thirteenth century and descended to the solid ground of textual criticism in the fifteenth. We have observed the varying effects of the Bible in turning men's minds now to historical reconstructions, and intermittently to powerful and awe-inspiring apocalyptic visions. We have seen how the unpredictable movements of peoples on a vast scale, and the inconspicuous efforts of translators in a frontier town in Spain, have changed the whole aspect of the Islamic problem. And then we have seen great systems of thought suddenly eclipsed and forgotten under the impact of a new turn in world events.

Most conspicuous to us is the inability of any of these systems of thought to provide a finally satisfying explanation of the phenomenon they had set out to explain—still less to influence the course of practical events in a decisive way. At a practical level, events never turned out either so well or so ill as the most intelligent observers predicted; and it is perhaps worth noticing that they never turned out better than when the worst was confidently predicted, or worse than when the best judges confidently expected a happy ending. Was there any progress? I must express my conviction that there was. Even if the solution of the problem remained obstinately hidden from sight, the statement of the problem became more complex, more rational, and more related to experience in each of the three stages of controversy which we have examined. The scholars who labored at the problem of Islam in the Middle Ages failed to find the solution they sought and desired; but they developed habits of mind and powers of comprehension which, in other men and in other fields, may yet deserve success.

INDEX

Saracens: in *Chanson de Roland*, 32; descent from Hagar, 17; etymology, 17n; supposed characteristics of, 29, 32; supposed origins in Old Testament, 15; supposed numbers of, 42–43

Sarah, wife of Abraham, 17, 18

Simon Semeonis, 70

Spain: Era of, 25n; importance in medieval thought, 19, 53, 88; Moslems in, 20–21, 104; translators in, 53, 87–88

Tartars, *see* Mongols

Thomas Aquinas, St., 55, 73

Toledo, 53

Uthred of Boldon, 76, 79, 82

Vienne, Council of, 72, 88

Vincent, St., 20n

Vincent of Beauvais, 78

Walter of Compiègne, *Otia de Machomete*, 30n, 31n

Walzer, Dr. R., 8

William of Malmesbury, 34–35

William of Rubroek, 47–52; account of his journey to Karakorum, 51; MSS of, 51n

William of Tripoli, 62–63

Wycliffe, John, 77–83; and Islamization of the West, 79–82